# ASSESSING CHILDREN'S WRITING

Sara Miller McCune founded SAGE Publishing in 1965 to support the dissemination of usable knowledge and educate a global community. SAGE publishes more than 1000 journals and over 800 new books each year, spanning a wide range of subject areas. Our growing selection of library products includes archives, data, case studies and video. SAGE remains majority owned by our founder and after her lifetime will become owned by a charitable trust that secures the company's continued independence.

Los Angeles | London | New Delhi | Singapore | Washington DC | Melbourne

# ASSESSING CHILDREN'S WRITING

## A BEST PRACTICE GUIDE FOR PRIMARY TEACHING

### KATE ALLOTT

Learning Matters
An imprint of SAGE Publications Ltd
1 Oliver's Yard
55 City Road
London EC1Y 1SP

SAGE Publications Inc.
2455 Teller Road
Thousand Oaks, California 91320

SAGE Publications India Pvt Ltd
B 1/I 1 Mohan Cooperative Industrial Area
Mathura Road
New Delhi 110 044

SAGE Publications Asia-Pacific Pte Ltd
3 Church Street
#10-04 Samsung Hub
Singapore 049483

© 2019 Kate Allott

Published in 2019

Editor: Amy Thornton
Senior project editor: Chris Marke
Marketing manager: Lorna Patkai
Cover design: Wendy Scott
Typeset by: C&M Digitals (P) Ltd, Chennai, India
Printed in the UK

**Library of Congress Control Number: 2018961093**

**British Library Cataloguing in Publication Data**

A catalogue record for this book is available from the British Library

ISBN 978-1-5264-4473-8
ISBN 978-1-5264-4474-5 (pbk)

At SAGE we take sustainability seriously. Most of our products are printed in the UK using responsibly sourced papers and boards. When we print overseas we ensure sustainable papers are used as measured by the PREPS grading system. We undertake an annual audit to monitor our sustainability.

# CONTENTS

# THE AUTHOR

**Kate Allott** is a lecturer in primary English at York St John University. She has also worked as a literacy consultant for North Yorkshire County Council, and as a regional adviser for the National Strategies Communication, Language and Literacy Development programme. Kate has published extensively in Primary English.

# INTRODUCTION

## The importance of writing assessment

Many teachers and parents are fascinated by children's writing. In addition to noting the impressive progress from the first wobbly marks on paper to the range and mastery of technical skills of many year 6 writers, children's work often gives an extraordinary window into their thinking and interests. In their writing, children are able to express their ideas and feelings, and demonstrate their knowledge and understanding. However, our fascination is greater if we have a sound understanding of all aspects of writing and of writing development. Without that knowledge, we really do not fully understand what we are looking at. More than this, we therefore do not know how to support children's future development.

For many children, getting to grips with written communication will be crucial to their success in education and in their careers. Writing matters. However, it has always been more difficult to assess than other areas of the curriculum. While it is relatively straightforward to decide if a child has used the past tense consistently, it is much more difficult to make a judgement on whether a piece of writing shows originality or a sense of audience. This book aims to support teachers and trainee teachers with the assessment of writing, and particularly assessment as part of the cycle of planning and teaching – in other words, assessment used formatively. If we are able to identify strengths in children's writing, and also areas for development, subsequent teaching is likely to be better focused and therefore more effective.

Accurate feedback is crucial to progress; studies of feedback reviewed in the *Teaching and Learning Toolkit* (n.d.), produced by the Education Endowment Foundation, Sutton Trust and Durham University, suggested that feedback has an extremely high impact compared with other teaching strategies.

The days of giving a piece of writing a tick and perhaps a comment such as 'good work' or 'lovely story', and correcting a few spelling mistakes, are long gone. Teachers spend a great deal of time marking children's writing, highlighting sections of the text which they consider to be particularly strong or in need of redrafting, writing encouraging comments, suggesting targets for future work. If this effort is to be productive, it is important to be knowledgeable about writing and writing development. But beyond this, Huot and Perry (2009) make the vital point that our focus needs to shift from marking children's writing to reading it. This may seem an odd point: how can one mark writing without reading it? But there is a real difference between reading in order to judge and reading as an ordinary reader. Teachers need to think as readers who expect to enjoy or learn from what they read, and then our response will be more helpful in developing effective writing.

# Issues in assessment

Assessment has been a controversial area in education for some time. The Carter Review (DoE, 2015a) indicated that assessment was the area most in need of improvement in initial teacher training, and its emphasis on the importance of good subject knowledge is also relevant to assessment. The Commission on Assessment without Levels (DoE, 2015b) identified variability in quality of training in assessment, during both initial teacher training and continuing professional development, as the biggest barrier to effective assessment practices in schools. More recently, the House of Commons Select Committee's report (2017) on primary assessment heard evidence from expert witnesses that there is not an effective system of training teachers in assessment procedures.

Bearne (2002) notes that writing is used to assess other subjects as well as being assessed in its own right, and a problem with assessing writing is that it is difficult, if not impossible, to separate content from style. Can a piece of writing be considered good if it is well written but the content is very limited or inaccurate? After all, it cannot be seen to have fulfilled its purpose, and that has to be a significant aspect of the assessment.

Another difficulty in assessing writing is that there is an inevitable element of subjectivity; The Cox Report, on the teaching of English in primary and secondary schools in England and Wales, stated:

> *The best writing is vigorous, committed, honest and interesting. We did not include these qualities in our statements of attainment because they cannot be mapped onto levels. Even so, all good classroom practice will be geared to encouraging and fostering these vital qualities.*

> (DES, 1989, para.17.31)

This statement could be interpreted as suggesting that the most important qualities of successful writing are the hardest to assess. Part of it is a question of personal preference; readers have very different tastes in fiction, and stories of the fierce debates among judges of fiction prizes (Raheem, 2012) suggest that the decision about what constitutes the 'best' writing is difficult. Even with non-fiction writing, readers will have different views about which texts are the most useful and interesting, but with fiction and poetry, where creativity and imagination become more significant, the difficulties are magnified. Creativity is a slippery concept and looking for evidence of creativity in writing is a difficult task: writers need to draw on their knowledge of the world and on their reading, while adding something original. Assessment of creativity in writing will be considered in Chapter 1. Brien (2012) points out that assessing writing is further complicated by the fact that what is considered a strength in one type of writing might not work in another genre, and that generic assessment tools cannot capture these aspects.

Even with aspects of writing that appear to be more straightforward to assess, there are difficulties. In punctuation, for example, how consistently do sentence boundaries need to be demarcated in order for us to conclude that the writer can do this successfully? All the time? Three-quarters of the time? The Standards and Testing Agency (2017a) even finds it necessary to give guidance on the meaning of 'some', 'many' and 'most' in relation to such judgements. Beyond this, how do we judge those aspects of punctuation that are a question of style rather than correctness – for example, the use of exclamation marks – which many writers for adult audiences would avoid? In addition to these questions, there is the wider question of whether the assessment is intended to be summative, making judgements of the quality of the writing, or formative and diagnostic, looking for areas that need development and trying to understand the difficulties the writer may have with writing. The pressure placed on teachers to track pupils' progress has led, perhaps inevitably, to a focus on summative assessment, and yet it may well be that a stronger focus on formative and diagnostic assessment would be more likely to result in good progress. The old adage that weighing the pig does not make it fatter is worth remembering here. If an overall judgement of writing is made, Richmond *et al.* (2017, p. 279) point out that *the Standards and Testing Agency acknowledges that we are still in the game of reducing a complex profile of achievement to a simple number.*

A further issue when teachers are assessing the writing of their own pupils is that of unconscious bias. They may be unaware that their own background and experience, or societal stereotypes, affect their views of pupils, and this can in turn result in too positive or too negative judgements of writing. The Education Endowment Foundation and Evidencebased.education's guide to assessment suggests that there tends to be bias against children with special educational needs and disability, children learning English as an additional language, those on free school meals and children with challenging behaviour. It may be difficult to reduce bias, but unless we acknowledge that it exists, we are unlikely to be able to tackle this problem.

# The importance of subject knowledge

In order to assess children's writing, a certain level of subject knowledge is needed by adults. Without this, we may recognise that some pieces of writing are successful and others less so, but be unable to say why and therefore unable to support children's writing development effectively. Technical vocabulary is useful in this context, for discussing writing with other professionals and with the pupils. Ofsted (2011), in a review of the impact of the Assessing Pupils' Progress initiative (QCDA and National Strategies, 2007), suggested that one of the benefits was that the materials gave teachers a common language for discussing their assessments. Subject knowledge is a particular issue with grammar, which many teachers and trainee teachers were not taught at school themselves, and which may seem fairly straightforward when applied to carefully designed examples in textbooks or tests, but which can be much more problematic when applied to 'real' language, including children's writing. Subject knowledge is also an issue for children trying to assess their own writing; if they find it difficult to identify fronted adverbials, for example, they may have used them without realising it, or may recognise some forms, such as adverbs or adverbial phrases, but not subordinate clauses acting as adverbials.

Chapter 6 therefore gives a step-by-step approach to analysing sentence structure. However, the need for secure subject knowledge to ensure secure assessment goes beyond grammar and the ability to, for example, recognise embedded clauses. In poetry, for example, everyone recognises rhyme but the importance of rhythm is sometimes neglected. Chapters 3, 4 and 5 therefore address subject knowledge specific to fiction, non-fiction and poetry in their consideration of children's writing of these text types. Chapter 1, Becoming a writer, focuses on children's developing understanding of writing, its purposes and processes, and their attitudes to it and sense of themselves as writers. These can be hugely important in their progress as writers. Chapter 2 looks at early writing and how we can assess children in the early stages of learning to write. Chapter 7 is the last chapter with a focus on composition, as it looks at children's vocabulary choices in writing. Chapters 8, 9 and 10 move on to consider the assessment of transcriptional aspects of writing – punctuation, spelling and hand-writing. Chapter 11 has a different focus: children's writing at home. While this may seem out of place in a book on assessing writing, it is interesting and useful to have some idea of how different children's writing at home may be, and what factors might cause any differences. Good practice in assessment in the Early Years Foundation Stage involves drawing on parents' and carers' knowledge of the child outside the educational setting (Standards and Testing Agency, 2017b); it seems appropriate to apply that principle to older children, so that we have a rounded picture of the child as a writer. It is also useful to reflect on how writing at home may be influenced by writing in school and vice versa. Finally, Chapter 12 addresses curriculum changes, statutory assessment of writing and moderation procedures, and national guidance.

## The writing samples

This book is based on examples of children's writing, but the names used are not the children's real names, except in one example where the child's attempts at writing her own name are included. The samples come from the full primary age range and include all the types of writing that children produce regularly in school. These are not exemplar pieces chosen to show the best of children's work; they may have been rushed, may not have been checked through by the writer, or may be incomplete. In other words, they represent the sort of writing that children produce and teachers mark on a daily basis. They were selected to show features of interest, with a focus on common issues in children's writing. They have, unless otherwise indicated, been transcribed with the original spelling and punctuation, but where the writers have made changes – for example, crossing out a word – the final version has been used. It is worth noting that it is easy to be unduly influenced by transcriptional aspects of writing (spelling, punctuation, handwriting) and that we should always seek to look beyond these to the content of the writing. At times, therefore, it can be helpful to consider examples where spelling and punctuation have been corrected, in order to free ourselves to consider organisation, content and style without being influenced by weak transcriptional skills. Transcripts, rather than the originals, have been used except in the chapter on handwriting, as the originals, some of which were written in pencil, were often not easy to read, and the effort needed to read them detracts from the reader's perception of the content. Following the analysis of each sample, next steps to support the child's development will be suggested.

## References

Bearne, E (2002) *Making Progress in Writing*. London: RoutledgeFalmer.

Brien, J (2012) *Teaching Primary English*. London: Sage.

Department for Education (2015a) *Carter Review of Initial Teacher Training*. London: Department for Education.

Department for Education (2015b) *Final Report of the Commission on Assessment without Levels*. London: Department for Education.

Department for Education and Science (DES) (1989) *The Cox Report: English for Ages 5 to 16*. London: HMSO.

Education Endowment Foundation, Sutton Trust and Durham University (n.d.) *Teaching and Learning Toolkit*. Available at: https://educationendowmentfoundation.org.uk/evidence-summaries/teaching-learning-toolkit (accessed 18 April 2018).

Education Endowment Foundation and Evidencebased.education (n.d.) *Assessing and Monitoring Pupil Progress*. Available at: https://educationendowmentfoundation.org.uk/resources/assessing-and-monitoring-pupil-progress/ (accessed 1 July 2018).

House of Commons Education Committee (2017) *Primary Assessment Report*. London: House of Commons.

Huot, B and Perry, J (2009) Towards a New Understanding for Classroom Writing Assessment. In Beard, R, Myhill, D, Riley, J and Nystrand, M (eds) *The Sage Handbook of Writing Development*. London: Sage, pp. 423–35.

Office for Standards in Education (Ofsted) (2011) *The Impact of the Assessing Pupils' Progress Initiative*. Manchester: Ofsted.

Qualifications and Curriculum Development Authority with National Strategies (2007) *Assessing Pupils' Progress*. London: DCSF.

Raheem, S (2012) Top Five Book Judging Controversies. *The Telegraph*, 25 January. Available at: www.telegraph.co.uk/culture/books/9038154/Top-five-book-judging-controversies.html (accessed 25 June 2018).

Richmond, J, Burn, A, Dougill, P, Raleigh, M and Traves, P (2017) *Curriculum and Assessment in English 3 to 11*. London: Routledge.

Standards and Testing Agency (2017a) *2018 Teacher Assessment Exemplification: English Writing*. London: Department for Education.

Standards and Testing Agency (2017b) *Early Years Foundation Stage Profile Handbook 2018*. London: Department for Education.

# 1
# BECOMING A WRITER

──────── IN THIS CHAPTER ────────

This chapter focuses on children's developing understanding of writing, its purposes and processes, and their attitudes to it and sense of themselves as writers. These can be hugely important in their progress as writers.

Becoming a writer is about far more than simply developing competence in writing. It involves, importantly, attitude to writing and understandings about writing. To a certain extent these are inter-dependent – for example, an older child who has not yet developed competence in writing is unlikely to have a positive attitude to writing. However, the opposite is not always true; some children write well but do not particularly enjoy writing, do not choose to write and are not interested in the writing process. They do not want to reflect on their own writing or rework it, and they do not find writing rewarding. Becoming a writer involves not only technical skills, but also a sense of oneself as a writer, sharing the struggles and satisfactions of writing with other writers. It involves awareness of writing as a process rather than simply being about a product; that although not every piece of writing will require this, some writing needs to be carefully planned and even researched. The writer also recognises that a first draft may require considerable reworking, and that the comments of others can be helpful. When the writing has been completed, writers consider it critically and know that this evaluation may be helpful in terms of their future development as writers. Bearne and Reedy (2018) also suggest that writers need to be able to balance composition and transcription, and creativity and structure, and this suggests a sophisticated awareness of the writing process.

## Audience and purpose

Bearne (2002) suggests that there tends to be a focus in assessment on technical aspects of writing rather than the writer's purpose and awareness of the intended audience, and she attributes this to teachers' anxieties about how to assess these less obvious features. If this means that children are not given feedback on these aspects, it is possible that they will not be able to discuss and develop them, and yet they are central to effective writing. As children develop confidence as writers, they are increasingly sure that they have something to write about, and have an increasingly accurate sense of their audience and audience needs. Perkins (2017) suggests that children know their writing is effective by the response they get to it, which tells them that it has met its purpose and understood its audience. This suggests that they need a 'real' audience for at least some of their writing. As they develop this awareness, they become more ready to tackle a range of writing activities and need less support in tackling new forms of writing; they are able to move from reading a few examples to producing their own quickly and successfully. They make their own decisions about their writing, and they are able to discuss their own and others' writing dispassionately and knowledgeably. They begin to use literary devices quite consciously, and are constantly aware of the effect of their writing, redrafting as they work – for example, to avoid repetition or to make their meaning clearer.

Whether children do see themselves as writers, and behave as writers, cannot be judged simply by the product of their writing. Observations of them engaged in writing and in discussions about writing provide valuable evidence. It is important to note whether children ever choose to write, and this will be returned to in Chapter 12, which considers children's writing at home. Assessment of children's attitudes to, and understanding of, writing matter because children who do not view themselves as writers, and do not engage with enthusiasm in writing activities, are less likely to make progress.

However, writing itself can give evidence of the writer's confidence and enjoyment. Consider a piece by Alekos, a pupil learning English as an additional language. Alekos was writing a reflection on his year at school, as all pupils did in his school. From a long piece, two extracts have been selected.

## CHILDREN'S WRITING

Alekos, year 5: Highlights of year 5

Where has time past I rember the first day I steped in to year 5 …

Drama week was fun we had a dama seshon where Jamila (my friend) was wearing a mask wich made her look sad and all the class had to chear her up. Let me tell you a little secret she was happy in the end.

## COMMENTARY

Alekos's introduction, with its rhetorical question, focuses on concepts of time – how quickly it seems to pass, how fresh memories can be and yet, as the long account shows, how much can happen in a year. These are thoughts that many adults have, and his elegiac note in this opening is often struck in adult writing. He is expressing genuine feelings. The second extract shows Alekos speaking directly to his audience, as if he is concerned that we are worried about Jamila – and yet we know, and he knows we know, that she is not really sad. The use of 'little' contributes to his reassuring tone, and 'happy in the end' has an echo of traditional stories. The 'sharing a secret' technique is a way of drawing readers in and making them feel they have a special relationship with the writer. It is probable that Alekos did not consciously select any of the techniques he uses here; he simply knows how to talk to people and we hear his voice very clearly. Authorial voice may be a somewhat difficult concept, but it should mean that the audience has a sense of the writer as a person, and we certainly have that here.

The reverse is also important – that the writer has a sense of the audience. Too often, writing in school does not give children that sense of who they are writing for and what the purpose of the writing is, and yet many of the important decisions that writers make about their writing depends on this understanding. The following example demonstrates this very clearly.

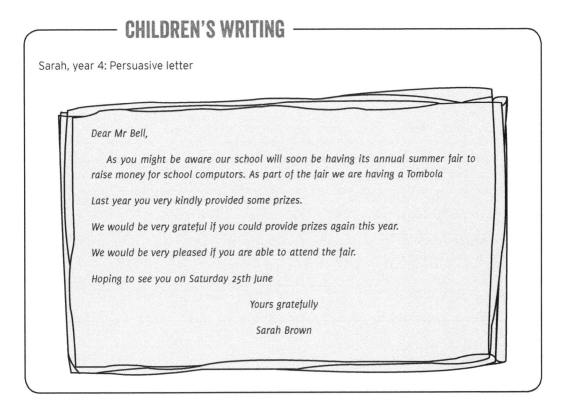

## CHILDREN'S WRITING

Sarah, year 4: Persuasive letter

Dear Mr Bell,

As you might be aware our school will soon be having its annual summer fair to raise money for school computors. As part of the fair we are having a Tombola

Last year you very kindly provided some prizes.

We would be very grateful if you could provide prizes again this year.

We would be very pleased if you are able to attend the fair.

Hoping to see you on Saturday 25th June

Yours gratefully

Sarah Brown

## COMMENTARY

Begging letters are always a challenge to writers, who are aware that they may be received with a sigh and some resentment rather than enthusiasm. Sarah does not know Mr Bell, but she can imagine his possible response to her letter. The right tone needs to be struck, and this is done successfully here through the use of modal verbs (would, might), the repeated use of the intensifier *very*, and vocabulary choice (kindly, grateful, gratefully, pleased, hoping). All of this suggests an appropriate level of uncertainty about the possible response – no one likes to be taken for granted – along with a reference to the donor's previous generosity – it is difficult not to live up to one's previous record – and the warm reception any donation would be given.

Becoming a successful writer is also dependent on knowledge of the world and being able to draw on this, process it and re-present it. This is true not only of non-fiction writing, where it can be difficult when assessing to separate out, for example, the child's knowledge of the subject from their writing skills, but also of fiction. Historical fiction, for example, depends on being able to present a convincing picture of life in a different age. Children may draw on knowledge gleaned from history lessons or from experiences outside school for this, but may also draw on fiction set in the past. The following example shows this: Molly is a keen reader of historical fiction and these extracts from her uncompleted story contain details drawn from her reading.

## CHILDREN'S WRITING

Molly, year 5: The horn

> It was early in the morning and Gertie rang the bell for breakfast. On the stairs was Grace, the breakfast maid, running as fast as she could, for Gertie wanted her breakfast and she had to be quick about everything, even the baby's breakfast … She had to come up seven flights of stairs to reach Gertie's bedroom and the mistress's bedroom was two flights of stairs up from Gertie's bedroom because she wanted some peace and quiet from the five children. The cook, Mrs Broom, was ordering about everybody in the servant hall …
>
> Gertie had a beautiful horse called Daisy it was a rocking horse …
>
> 'Now be off with you! In five minutes we are going to leave. I will get the housemaid to ask Edward to drive us there.'

## COMMENTARY

It is unlikely that the mistress would have a bedroom on a higher floor than her children's, but generally Molly has developed a strong sense of life in a wealthy family in the past and has used this to good effect in her own story. This can be seen in details of the story, such as the bells to summon servants and the vocabulary she uses, such as 'mistress', but she has also used language such as the conjunction 'for' and the phrase 'be off with you', which give a sense of the past.

The assessment of writing has to consider the overall impact of the work – whether it meets its purpose and the needs of its audience. This, after all, is how writing generally is judged. In adult life, when non-fiction texts are read, they are judged by how useful or interesting the information they contain is and how clearly it is communicated. It is stating the obvious to say that writing is about communication, but it is apparent that some writers are much more effective communicators than others, and this is so for adults as well as children. Lesser considerations may be how well the text reads or possibly also whether it entertains as well as informs. When adults read fiction, they judge it by how engrossed in it they become, what emotions and thoughts it provokes, and also possibly by the beauty of the language or by striking imagery, which makes the reading a more satisfying experience. There is also a sense of truth in writing – that a character in fiction or an argument in persuasive writing convinces us. Writing is both an art and a craft: writers use a range of skills, as any craftsman does, but good writing has qualities that can be hard to pin down and assess – originality, freshness, humour, honesty. Becoming a writer involves not only developing those skills, but may also involve incorporating those qualities.

# Creativity

Writing – of fiction and poetry – was traditionally seen as one of the creative arts in primary school, along with art, dance and music. It is difficult, however, to be creative without the skills and knowledge that allow one to realise one's creative ideas, so we might expect more evidence of creativity in older writers, who have good skills and are able to consciously select and use writing techniques. It is perhaps even more difficult to attempt to assess creativity, but if we think it is important, then the attempt should be made. Grant Wiggins's rubric for assessing creativity, which consists of a six-point scale, is helpful here, and the following scale is based on his original, using the aspects most relevant to writing.

| **6 Unusually creative** |
| --- |
| • New, striking and effective ideas and language are used. |
| • Techniques are used very effectively, without being overdone. |
| • Ideas may be combined in original ways and rules may be deliberately broken. |
| • Striking details and touches make the writing vivid. |
| • There is a mixture of explicit 'telling' and hints. |
| • The work generates strong responses from readers. |
| **5 Highly creative** |
| • New ideas and approaches are used effectively. |
| • A personal style is evident. |
| • Ideas and materials are combined in new ways. |
| • The work generates a lively response from readers. |
| **4 Creative** |
| • New ideas are used. |
| • There are imaginative touches. |
| • There is a distinctive style, but this is not consistently maintained. |
| • The writing takes some risks. |
| • The audience is mostly engaged. |

*(Continued)*

(Continued)

| **3 Somewhat creative** |
| --- |
| • Familiar approaches used, writing is 'safe'. |
| • Some ideas taken from elsewhere but not well integrated. |
| • The writing mixes different approaches but lacks coherence, or is competent and coherent but lacks spark. |
| **2 Not very creative** |
| • The work offers little that is new. |
| • Writing lacks a personal voice or style. |
| • The work mixes different approaches in an incoherent way. |
| • The writing is polished rather than imaginative. |
| **1 Uncreative** |
| • The writing follows a model uncritically. |
| • Work is predictable and lacks a personal touch. |
| • There is an absence of vivid ideas and feelings. |

*Source*: Adapted from Grant Wiggins (2012).

The scale suggests that while technical mastery facilitates creativity, it does not ensure it, and even children in the early stages of writing may show genuine creativity in the way they combine ideas. The following example demonstrates this; it is a piece of child-initiated writing from a pupil in a reception class.

## CHILDREN'S WRITING

Megan, reception: To do list

a list of thingcs

to bo wal lm ote

Look ote for the

Jaiaurnd

for ayoor supa

there is the

Wulfcs in the

luvn

(A list of things to do while I'm out

Look out for the giant

For your supper there is the wolfs in the oven.)

The list combines in an original way the nature of everyday family communications with material from fairy stories.

## Attitude to writing

Bearne (2002, p. 22) identifies the following as characteristics of successful writers.

- Greater willingness to write.

- Greater attention to detail.

- More fluent and regular handwriting.

- Greater fluency leading to greater confidence (and vice versa).

- Choosing to write at home/in the writing area.

- Learning what it means to 'be a writer' – which is different from learning to write.

Of these characteristics, handwriting is the focus of Chapter 10. Chapter 11 addresses writing at home, and this links with willingness to write and also raises the question of whether writing can be viewed as a choice in school once children move on from Foundation Stage. Increasingly, as children move through the primary years every moment of the day is programmed, and although there may be

## IN THE CLASSROOM

When observing, points to note include the following.

- Do children appear to react positively when a writing task is proposed (e.g. smile and listen attentively to instructions, or sigh and look anxious)?

*(Continued)*

(Continued)

- Do children begin on writing tasks immediately (note that this might include thinking about or discussing what they plan to write) or avoid the task using strategies such as pencil sharpening, chatting, or slow copying of dates and titles?
- Do children appear absorbed in their writing, or are they easily distracted, looking around, engaging in off-task behaviours?
- Is any talk during writing related to the task or off-task?
- Are children keen to complete writing tasks (e.g. asking if they can finish work if they have run out of time), or are they unconcerned about unfinished pieces?
- Are children happy to return to pieces of writing to improve and check them?
- Do children appear to enjoy sharing their writing with others?

substantial amounts of time given to writing, these will be fixed periods with tightly constrained tasks and expectations, even though we know that giving writers choices can be beneficial (Ofsted, 2003). Children's willingness to write can be assessed both by observation and by discussion with children. These can give an indication of which children are willing or even keen to write, and which are reluctant, and also of whether a class as a whole is more or less enthusiastic about writing compared with, for example, mathematics, art or physical education.

The child's voice is important. Children spend a great deal of time at school writing and they know that teachers think it is important; we will be better placed to support them as writers if we know what they think about writing.

## IN THE CLASSROOM

Questions for children might include the following.

- When it's time for writing at school, what do you think?
- Where do you get your ideas for writing from?
- Do you do any writing at home? What sort? When, where?
- Which do you enjoy most – writing at home or writing at school?
- What makes someone a good writer?
- What happens to your writing when it's finished?
- What do you like to happen to your writing when it's finished?
- What sort of writing do grown-ups do?
- Why do you need to be able to write?
- Do you think you're a good writer? Why do you think that?

- What can teachers do to help you get better at writing?
- What kinds of writing do you enjoy doing most?
- What is the hardest thing about writing?

Responses are often revealing. Children may know that writing is seen as important without any clear sense of why it is and what part it plays in the adult world. In answer to the question, 'Why do you need to be able to write?', Connor, Year 2, said that 'You need to be able to otherwise you probably – not have much stuff to help you.' It is quite likely that he had never considered this question before, and it might be helpful if adults talked about the purposes of literacy with children regularly. Leila, Year 3, commented that it was important 'if you wanted to be an author when you're older'. Frank, Year 6, said, 'Grown-ups don't do much writing unless they're teachers.' He added that it wouldn't really matter if one were unable to write. None of these children had a clear sense of how the adults they knew best used writing, Leila stating that 'They just write down notes and stuff', while Connor suggested that 'Maybe they might write a card to their friends or if they're a teacher they might write your learning intention'. Connor characterised adult writing as 'fast grown-up writing', and it is possible that unless prompted, children do not think of writing using computers and other technological devices as writing. Nor, of course, do many children see their parents writing as part of their jobs, and even when parents do work at home, it is likely to be computer-based and probably in a separate room. It could be helpful for children to have a clearer idea of the important place of writing in many adult lives, so that it is not seen as essentially a school activity.

Children's sense of themselves as writers can be limited by what they believe to be important to teachers. Asked if he saw himself as a good writer, Connor responded, 'Well, on my train maps I sometimes rush a bit, but when I'm doing stories I try my very hardest.' It appeared that in his mind, effort and carefulness were the important factors in producing good writing, even though he was referring to writing done at home. He also explained that a good writer is someone who has good letter formation and knows how to spell lots of words. This was echoed by James, also in Year 2, who was very clear that he was the second best writer in his class because a girl did better on spelling tests than he did. Wray (1993) suggested that children's emphasis on the importance of transcriptional aspects of writing do become less marked as they moved through Key Stage 2, and might well reflect their own anxieties rather than their teachers' preoccupations. Leila had a very different sense of how to judge one's success as a writer, as shown in this response to the same question: 'I would say in the middle. About five people are better than me. Certain people get theirs read out every time. They were the first two to get handwriting pens.' She also was clear about how to become a better writer, and this suggested a broader view of writing: 'I would say you need to write a couple of days a week and read more books so you get more imagination so you don't have to think for an hour, so you know what it's going to be about.' Her sense of the importance of ideas and content are evident. The difference between the children is reflected in their ideas about how teachers might help them to write better: Connor suggested simply that 'They might tell you how to form letters or how to spell words', while Leila's views reflected her own needs as well as her sense of her teacher's priorities: 'I would say give more time to write so I can do longer stories and give all the details. If I've just got half an hour I have to do simple stuff.' Prompted to say what her teacher actually did do to help her improve, she added, 'She explains what we have to do. And corrections – say, we need more adjectives or if we don't have adverbs we need more adverbs. And you should do more similes.'

Children's understanding of what makes for good writing reflects what they are taught about this: Elliot, a Year 6 pupil, explained that 'she teaches us about personification, alliteration, similes, metaphors and all them'; he added that he knew his writing was good if he had 'crossed Ts and done personification and everything Ms G. says we should do', and that she helped him by giving him a folder with 'uplevelled words'. James found it much more difficult to explain what made a story a good story: 'It would be good if I would be doing adjectives, some nouns maybe if it's a thing where we have nouns. I'd write the setting, maybe the person in it, what happened.'

# The writing process

Children's understanding of the writing process is also variable: both Elliot and Leila were sure that their ideas for stories came from other stories, though their thinking on the planning stage was not clear. Leila explained, 'If it's stories definitely I know what to write, so then I don't stop to think. Should I put lots and lots of adjectives on, should I think about descriptive language or should I focus on handwriting? Stories can be very long, but others are short because there's not much to write. Poems are really good; I have to think what shall I put at the end of the sentence [rhyming words].' Her comments reveal a mixture of a concern about needing to decide what to write quickly so that she has as much time for writing as possible, and also an awareness of what her teacher is likely to be looking for.

The writing process involves starting with a sense of the audience and purpose of the writing, and therefore its form. Children develop a sense of what constitutes a 'real' purpose for writing and therefore a meaningful form. Sadie, a Year 6 pupil, for example, dismissed 'boring' writing such as character descriptions because 'you never find them at the start of books'. She had noticed that real fiction is unlikely to contain lengthy and detailed descriptions of the main characters, and therefore rejected them as worthwhile tasks. She was, however, happy to write diary entries in the role of a character from a story, perceiving these as similar to stories she had read in diary format.

Some children seem to have a very limited sense of the importance of the later stages of the writing process, often being reluctant to redraft their work and also to check it through. Connor, explaining that the hardest thing about writing is 'Making sure you don't get your words in the wrong order and also making sure you don't do something that doesn't make sense', knew that the way to address these potential problems is 'by reading your writing after'. He added gloomily, 'I'm not very keen on it.' Despite the emphasis on providing positive feedback, children seem to see feedback as being essentially negative: Sadie explained: 'Sometimes we swap with a partner. I feel scared they're going to put something bad. [Is it ever helpful to you?] A tiny bit helpful.' She described the next part of the process in the following way: 'The teacher checks it, then says you need to check it again because there are errors in it. [What sort of errors?] Crossing Ts, punctuation.'

The work is then marked and even if she feels the overall feedback is good, 'there's always a bit of pink [highlighter pen] – I've done something wrong'. In spite of the highlighting of specific pieces of text, Sadie comments that she does not like going back to improve her writing 'because you don't know which bit she's not happy with'.

The use of pink and green highlighter pens (practice in different schools varies as to what each colour denotes) appears to be widespread, and although the intention is positive – to encourage children by noting good features and to suggest parts that could usefully be revised – it often seems to be seen in a negative way by children. James, for example, explained the process in his Year 2 class: 'They mark it green if there's any problems and pink if it's fine, basically. When it's green I just go into my work and if we're doing a check walk I have to sort it out and when I finally get it right I would get a pink tick and that means I don't have to do any more of that sort of thing.'

There is a distinct feeling of relief at the end of his comments, and again a sense that this is about putting right things that are wrong, rather than considering options for improving aspects that might be weaker than the rest of the piece. It may be that there is a confusion between redrafting, editing and proofreading; this is particularly likely to be so if children are mainly asked to alter spelling and punctuation rather than content, sentence structure or vocabulary.

As children develop as writers, they should learn to assess their own writing realistically in order to know how to improve it. Andrade *et al.* (2010) found that older pupils benefited from developing their own assessment criteria by analysing successful examples of the type of writing they were about to produce; although the criteria they produced were similar to those given to the control group, the control group performed less well. The National Curriculum programme of study (DfE, 2013) includes self-assessment in all years, but does not explicitly state that children should be involved in developing success criteria. The programme includes the following.

Year 1: rereading what they have written to check that it makes sense.

Year 2: make simple additions, revisions and corrections to their own writing by:

- evaluating their writing with the teacher and other pupils;
- rereading to check that their writing makes sense and that verbs to indicate time are used correctly and consistently, including verbs in the continuous form;
- proof-reading to check for errors in spelling, grammar and punctuation [for example, ends of sentences punctuated correctly].

Years 3 and 4 – evaluate and edit by:

- assessing the effectiveness of their own and others' writing and suggesting improvements;
- proposing changes to grammar and vocabulary to improve consistency, including the accurate use of pronouns in sentences.

Years 5 and 6 – evaluate and edit by:

- assessing the effectiveness of their own and others' writing;

- proposing changes to vocabulary, grammar and punctuation to enhance effects and clarify meaning;

- ensuring the consistent and correct use of tense throughout a piece of writing;

- ensuring correct subject and verb agreement when using singular and plural, distinguishing between the language of speech and writing and choosing the appropriate register.

It may be that putting evaluation and editing together causes difficulties, because the distinction between them is lost and editing is emphasised at the expense of the more difficult, but arguably more important, process of evaluation (and potentially redrafting). This can be seen in the following example, which is first simply edited for spelling and punctuation errors, but then redrafted to organise the content more effectively.

## CHILDREN'S WRITING

Sam, year 4: A letter to a character

The cubed under the stairs

4 Privit drive

Little Whinging

Surrey

*Dear Harry,*

*Your invited to Hogwats for a term of witchy craft and wizadory magic, and flying lesons. Catch the 9 and 3/4 at 9:40 don't be late. Hogwarts is full of secrets and magic also some lessons that are about flying objects. Hadgrid will meet you in the station don't get lost will you. Hadgrid brought you to the Dursleys, oh yes next Monday come to the station dont forget to get a wand, a cloack, a cat, owl or frog, robes, a hat. So all of this is what your doing for centerys.*

*Proffeser Dumbuldor*

*P.S. don't go on the 3rd floor it's forbbidon we arnt mean or enithing it's death or live thats your choice death or live.*

*Spelling and punctuation corrected*

*You're invited to Hogwarts for a term of witchy craft and wizardry magic, and flying lessons. Catch the 9 and ¾ at 9:40; don't be late. Hogwarts is full of secrets and magic, also some lessons that are about flying objects. Hadgrid will meet you in the station – don't get lost, will you? Hadgrid brought you to the Dursleys. Oh yes, next Monday come to the station. Don't forget to get a wand, a cloak, a cat, owl or frog, robes, a hat. So all of this is what you're doing for centuries.*

*Redrafted version*

*You are invited to Hogwarts for a term of witchy craft and wizardry magic, and flying lessons. Hogwarts is full of secrets and magic; also there are lessons about flying objects. Next Monday come to the station and catch the train from platform 9 ¾ at 9:40; don't be late. Hagrid, who brought you to the Dursleys, will meet you in the station; don't get lost, will you? Don't forget to get a wand, a cloak, a cat, owl or frog, robes, and a hat. So all of this is what you're doing for centuries.*

Even when the spelling and punctuation have been corrected, there are issues with how the letter is structured. Moving content around produces a more logical sequence.

# Conclusion

We will look finally at a piece of writing from an older pupil to seek evidence of his development as a writer.

## CHILDREN'S WRITING

Marcus, year 6: Witches' immulsion

Craving the sleek, soft web of a blood desiring shelob (a colossal arachnid)? Or the bleeding, splintered hand of a foolish delinquent? Perhaps even the life energy which only the perfect demon spawn can contain? Well look no further than 'Red's rich immulsion' which makes what you desire appear right in front of you; I'm sure you'll agree that this is the perfect way to stop you searching for days on end for just the right riches you are looking to acquire!

*(Continued)*

(Continued)

You will require:

- A black iron cauldreon (Preferably durable)
- A vintage wooden spoon (unbreakable)

In order to efficiently conjure the immulsion successfully you must follow the intricate – yet simple – steps:

One: Before you begin, remember to add a singular drop of your blood to make sure the potion verifies it's you – this is the case due to others failing to keep it safe from bandits/thieves/other magic users. Additionally, make sure you are atop a hill, below a blue moon – preferably a full moon.

Two: Locate an illusive poison dart frog to withdraw the poison for the perfect spell …

Three: Hunt down a Black Widow and take part of their web – in order to add the most important piece of the puzzle!

Four: Now – the final ingredient – the bleeding hand of a bear: a major part of your success! Once you have acquired all of these ingredients place them in a cauldron (hopefully 300 degrees C) and use the ladel/spoon to mix them!

Now – if the shape of your desired target is changing, your spell has worked flawlessly meaning you're smarter than the average spell caster/potion conjurer! Listen to one of our follower's quotes: "This potion has made my life easier as now I don't have to go miles away from my home to go from rags to riches!" – it's almost as if it was made by magic!

## COMMENTARY

Marcus seems to have enjoyed this writing. He has been able to draw on his knowledge of different forms of writing and to combine them. He starts with gusto, three questions drawing in the audience, and uses a wide range of details appropriate to horror writing – blood, spiders, moonlight, and so on. The writing reads well because Marcus uses devices such as alliteration effectively. He scatters exclamation marks around freely, suggesting the over-excited tone of much advertising material. He includes some little jokes – the 'preferably durable' cauldron, and the 'intricate yet simple' steps. He is playing with the genre, writing to entertain, and he does so with confidence.

Becoming a writer, then, involves a complex range of skills and understandings. Children may see themselves as writers from very early on, or still not feel comfortable in the role by the end of primary school. They need to develop a clear sense of audience and purpose, and be familiar with a range of different forms. They need to be able to plan, draft and revise their writing. They need to be able to select and organise content, and adapt their language as appropriate. They should learn to evaluate their own writing honestly and carefully, preferably in relation to criteria they have developed themselves through analysis of successful examples. As they develop as writers, they should have the confidence to experiment and take risks. We should also hope that while they recognise that writing is not always easy, it can give them a great sense of satisfaction and pride.

# References

Andrade, HL, Du, Y and Mycek, K (2010) Rubric-referenced Self-assessment and Middle School Students' Writing. *Assessment in Education: Principles, Policy and Practice, 17*: 199–214.

Bearne, E (2002) *Making Progress in Writing*. London: RoutledgeFalmer.

Bearne, E and Reedy, D (2018) *Teaching Primary English: Subject Knowledge and Classroom Practice*. Abingdon: Routledge.

Department for Education (DfE) (2013) *The 2014 Primary National Curriculum in England*. Eastleigh: Shurville Publishing.

Ofsted (2003) *Yes He Can: Schools Where Boys Write Well*. Manchester: Ofsted.

Perkins, M (2017) *Observing Primary Literacy*. London: Sage.

Wiggins, G (2012) *Rubric for Assessing Creativity*. Available at: https://grantwiggins.files.wordpress. com/2012/02/creative.pdf (accessed 12 March 2018).

Wray, D (1993) What do Children Think about Writing? *Educational Review, 45*(1): 67–77.

# 2
# EARLY WRITING DEVELOPMENT

┌─────────── IN THIS CHAPTER ───────────┐

This chapter looks at early writing and how we can assess children in the early stages of learning to write.
└────────────────────────────────────────┘

Children arrive in nursery or school at different points in their development in all areas of learning, including writing. They are likely to have had very different experiences in their early years, and to show varied levels of interest and motivation in relation to writing and mark-making in general. Some children develop an early and consistent interest in mark-making, and may engage in the activity on a daily basis and even several times a day or for long periods. Others may engage with enthusiasm for a while and then move on to other interests. Others may seem to show little interest at all. Some children come from homes where mark-making materials are constantly available to them, and where adults are interested in their mark-making and involve them in mark-making activities such as signing greetings cards; others may not have these early experiences. The variation in early interest and experience is likely to result in different levels of understanding of writing and its purposes, and also different skill levels, particularly pencil grip and pencil control.

## Early mark-making

A crucial step in writing development is the recognition that drawing and writing are different, and that there is a category of marks that carry meaning in a different way from pictures. In the early stages, these marks bear the same relationship to 'real' writing that babbling bears to oral language. They may look like writing and the child may attribute meaning to them, but without having the understanding that writing represents the sounds of spoken language. These early attempts often involve either horizontal lines of zigzag or wavy movements, which draw on children's knowledge of adult joined script, or letter-like symbols that may draw more on print script, whether modelled by adults for the children or seen in printed texts. However, an interest in writing may quickly lead to the recognition of particular marks as having significance, and so very rapidly real letters may begin to feature in children's mark-making. The letters of their own names and of the names of people close to them are likely to be the first to appear, possibly as a result of adults modelling the writing of their names for them, or labelling their paintings, models and so on in pre-school settings, so that they can be identified later.

The five samples that follow show several of these features; all of them come from the same child and were produced between the ages of 3 years 3 months and 4 years 2 months. It is important to note that all of them were child-initiated.

*Figure 2.1*

## COMMENTARY

Having seen adults write her name on her drawings and paintings, Meg (3:6 years) has written her name on her own drawing (see Figure 2.1). As the following sample shows, at this stage even the left–right orientation is not secure and the name is written vertically (see Figure 2.2). It can also be noted that the letters do not appear to be in the right sequence (Mge rather than Meg) and that while the 'e' is better formed than in the first sample, where it has a very long entry stroke, the 'g' which was correctly formed in the first sample is incomplete in the second. Letter formation is a huge challenge to early writers.

*Figure 2.2*

It is worth pointing out that the task of learning to write their name is much harder for some children that for others – a child called Will, for example, has to learn only three letters, all of which are composed of straight lines, whereas a Christopher would have to learn nine letters, including anti-clockwise 'o' and 'c' and clockwise 'p' and 'r'; the difficult 's' and both ascenders ('h' and 't') and a descender in 'p'. This perhaps calls into question how meaningful the writing of their own names is as a measure of progress: a development statement for 40–60 months in Development Matters (Early Education, 2012) says that children should be able to write their own name, but this is a far higher hurdle for some than for others.

The significance of the name is shown again in the following sample (see Figure 2.3), where the initial letter is repeated over and over. It is interesting that children will sometimes spontaneously practise a skill they want to master with great persistence, but may be very reluctant to engage with adult-initiated practice. It is also true that parents and carers often place a great deal of importance on name-writing, and will encourage it, model it and be delighted when the child is successful, much as they were when the first spoken word was produced. An issue for teachers in the early years is that parents may teach children to write their names using capital letters, thinking that this will be easier for them. Retraining them to use lower case letters needs to be done sensitively and may take some time.

## COMMENTARY

At the same time as learning to write her own name, the child often made marks that looked like writing, but which did not communicate meaning. There were some recognisable letters, but these

*Figure 2.3*

were not being used to represent sounds. However, this was evidence of significant learning: the child recognised the difference between drawing and writing, and knew that the marks 'said' something. She often responded confidently when asked the question 'What does your writing say?' This is an important stage and children's achievements should be valued.

*Figure 2.4*

## COMMENTARY

Here, the letter-like marks appear to be grouped into words and are clearly a caption for the picture (see Figure 2.4). An upper-case A can be identified.

*Figure 2.5*

## COMMENTARY

Eight months later, the child was still at the same stage of writing development. In this example (see Figure 2.5), there is a mixture of separate letters (upper-case M and H can be seen) and continuous line scribble which represents joined writing. Observing adults' writing, children are likely to see both printed and joined script, so it is hardly surprising when their own writing uses both forms. It is very important to recognise that a child who spends many months at this stage is not necessarily 'stuck' or making no progress, and we should support development sensitively. Trying to rush a child on to learning letters and attempting to encode can result in a loss of interest and motivation.

When assessing early mark-making, there is much more to consider than what appears on the paper. It is important to observe children during the process, as much information can only be gathered in this way. Considerations such as their posture and pencil grip, but also what they say (if anything) while mark-making, and also how long they spend and whether it is a solitary or shared activity, are all vital to building up a picture of the young writer. A checklist such as the one that follows can be a helpful prompt, ensuring that assessment focuses on all aspects of writing.

## IN THE CLASSROOM

### A framework for analysing early writing (mark-making)

The framework suggests what to look for in children's mark-making in the EYFS. Note that evidence of many important aspects of children's mark-making can only be gathered through observation and possibly through talking with the child.

## Purpose and meaning

- Is the child able to compose texts orally (e.g. captions for pictures, signs and notices, messages in cards)?
- Does the child distinguish between different types of marks (e.g. pictures and writing)?
- Does the child give meaning to marks (e.g. tell others what their marks 'say')?
- Does the child show awareness of writing for different purposes (e.g. describing marks as a list or a letter)?
- Does the child make connections between mark-making and other activities (e.g. making labels for models he/she has made, making signs and notices for the role play area)?
- Are marks grouped into 'words'?
- Are marks arranged in horizontal rows and written from left to right?

## Knowledge of letters and sounds

- Does the child recognise any letters (name or corresponding phoneme)?
- Does the child show an interest in letters – for example, recognising letters that are in his or her own name?
- Is the child able to hear any individual phonemes within words and, if so, which (initial, final, medial)?
- Does the child produce any recognisable letters?

## Handwriting

- Does the child have a mature pencil grip?
- Can the child control the pencil to produce, for example, straight lines and circles?
- Does the child use appropriate pressure when using mark-making tools?
- Does the child produce letter-like shapes or 'writing-like' scribble?

## Attitude

- Does the child choose to engage in mark-making activities and persist with them?
- Does the child show an interest in writing generally (e.g. asking adults about what they are writing)?

The framework is best used to assess the child's mark-making generally, using a range of samples and observations.

A more detailed analysis of a single sample, however, can tell us a great deal about the writer, as the following example shows.

---
## CHILDREN'S WRITING
---

Ruth, 3:8 years: family portrait

## COMMENTARY

This is a family portrait, with six or possibly seven human figures (the one second from the left seems to have two heads). The central figure is the most detailed, with tears, plaited hair, arms, hands, navel and clothes represented. The writing is horizontal and consists of a series of separate letter-like marks, with no spaces to group the marks into 'words'. There are two lines of writing above the picture, with attempts at the child's name at the top of the page, under the left-hand figure and beside the central one. It could be that these indicate which figure represents the child herself, and also a signature marking authorship of the work. Spelling of the name is not consistent – two attempts begin with Ru, but the third seems to have been written from right to left, and the R is followed by the 't'. Among the marks in the two lines of 'writing' can be seen several upper-case As, several 'u's (without the final downstroke), several 'n's, some with the initial downstroke, a reversed 'h', two 'c's and several 'o's, some with short strokes bisecting the circle. There are also three marks that could be reversed '3's. The marks are of a fairly uniform size and the smoothness of both straight strokes and curves indicates good pencil control. There are some other marks of interest: above the second figure from the left are two marks, which may have been formed by turning the paper on its side to fit them in; if this is so, they suggest an 'l' and an 's'. Some of the marks have been underlined and on the lower line a number have dots underneath them. It is not clear what this might have been intended to indicate; as she had not encountered the phonics 'sound button' activity, this is not a likely explanation. Finally, the question mark and exclamation mark on the right-hand side of the paper should be noted. This suggests a keen interest in print and a recognition that these marks are significant and have something in common.

We can summarise this analysis by saying that the writer:

- demonstrates interest in print and in writing;

- has some understanding of the purpose of writing (labels, captions);

- is beginning to be able to write her own first name;

- can produce a number of recognisable letters, both upper and lower case;

- knows that writing is horizontal and consists of a variety of different letters;

- knows that writing includes other significant marks in addition to letters – e.g. punctuation marks, underlining.

We can also state that the writer does not yet group marks into words and that she does not yet use letters to represent phonemes in words. It is important to remember that Ruth's interest in writing has been developed and sustained by a rich literacy environment, and that her continued development can best be supported through this provision, rather than through an early move to formal teaching.

# Cracking the alphabetic code

The move from this pre-phonic stage to the phonic stage, where letters are actually used to represent at least some of the sounds heard in words, may be a sudden jump forward rather than a gradual change. When a child begins to work out, or is taught, the alphabetic code and understands that the basis of the English writing system is that letters represent sounds – and also has knowledge of at least some of the basic phoneme/grapheme (sound/letter) correspondences – this is a transformation. Instead of their writing having meaning only for them, it begins to communicate meaning to others. While some children may begin to make this advance before they begin formal education, for most it will happen as they embark on a programme of systematic phonics teaching, during the reception year. This is a hugely exciting development for children, teachers and parents. In the past, phonics was often introduced later on and much more slowly, and phonics teaching tended to be limited to the simple code (one letter makes one sound) and a few digraphs such as 'ch', 'th', 'sh', 'oo' and 'ee'. The pace of phonics teaching in most schools today means that many children move quite quickly from not being able to encode to being able to hear most or all phonemes in words, and knowing at least one way of representing each of the phonemes they use – the expectation for the end of the reception year. This means they can generally write anything they want to (long words can, of course, present a particular challenge). In the past, models of spelling development such as Gentry's (1982) indicated that between the pre-alphabetic phase, where written symbols did not represent sounds in words, and full alphabetic writing, in which every phoneme is represented, came a partial alphabetic writing phase, in which only some phonemes were represented – typically prominent ones, such as the first and last in the word. In this phase, children might write H D for Humpty Dumpty, or 'I am scd' for 'I am scared'. However, the emphasis over recent years on daily systematic phonics teaching from the beginning of the reception year may have shortened this phase, or even resulted in children representing all the phonemes, at least in simple consonant, vowel, consonant (CVC) words, from the start.

## IN THE CLASSROOM

In assessing children's ability to encode, several questions need to be considered.

- Is the child representing all the phonemes in the word?
- Is the child representing each phoneme with an appropriate grapheme?
- Are some graphemes included which do not match a phoneme in the word?

The following three examples show a range of achievement. The children, all in the same reception class, were writing their favourite nursery rhyme on the computer.

## CHILDREN'S WRITING

Keira wrote: Insi winsi spade

## COMMENTARY

Keira has heard every phoneme in each word, including adjacent consonants in all three words, and has matched each to an appropriate grapheme apart from the vowels in the last word, where she has used 'a' for the long vowel phoneme /igh/, although it may be that 'a' is a reasonable representation of the way she pronounces the word. She has also had difficulty with the unstressed vowel phoneme at the end of the word, which can be represented in many different ways. It may be that her use of 'e' shows a memory of the visual appearance of the word.

## CHILDREN'S WRITING

Jack wrote: Litl mis mufit

Jack has represented all the phonemes except the unstressed vowel phoneme in 'little' and has used appropriate graphemes for each phoneme. It is worth noting that all the vowels in this sample are short, so we do not know how Jack might have attempted to represent any long vowel phonemes. It should also be noted that none of the words contain adjacent consonants.

## CHILDREN'S WRITING

Ben wrote: ins wins spbdr

## COMMENTARY

Ben has heard most of the phonemes in the three words and has represented most of them with appropriate grapheme choices. He has not heard the final vowel phoneme in the first two words, and in 'spider' he does not seem to have heard either vowel phoneme, although it could be that the 'r' at the end, as with Keira's 'e', shows a partial memory of the visual appearance of the word and how the final vowel phoneme is represented. The 'b' is a puzzle, and this could simply mean that he has at first chosen the wrong letter to represent the /d/, or that he has had two attempts at representing the /p/ phoneme, which is almost the same sound as /b/.

The analysis shows the enormous achievement of these three reception children. Within a few months of starting school they have learned to segment words into their constituent phonemes, hold those phonemes in their working memory, in the right order, and find a suitable grapheme to represent each one. Their writing can now be read; they can use the alphabetic code successfully to communicate meaning.

## IN THE CLASSROOM

There is much more to writing than encoding, and children need to be able to bring together a number of different skills and understandings at this stage, including the following.

- Phonological awareness: the child must be able to hear at least some phonemes in words. Many listening games and activities will help to develop this awareness, as will singing and saying nursery rhymes, listening to stories in rhyme and language play.
- Knowledge of phoneme/grapheme (sound/letter) correspondences: some of this may be acquired informally - for example, through discussion of letters in the child's name or other significant words - or it may be acquired through planned phonics teaching.
- Pencil control: this is best developed through drawing, which is pleasurable and purposeful for the child.
- Letter formation: this is best taught systematically once children have developed good pencil control.
- Understanding of the purposes and value of writing, and forms of writing: this is best acquired through adult modelling and widespread opportunities for mark-making within role-play activities.

Some of these areas are discussed in other chapters – phonological awareness and knowledge of phoneme–grapheme correspondences in Chapter 9 (Spelling); pencil control and letter formation in Chapter 10 (Handwriting), understanding of the purposes and value of writing in Chapter 1 (Becoming a writer), and knowledge of different forms of writing in Chapter 4, which shows the range of text types produced independently by a child in the Early Years Foundation Stage. However, it is important not to lose sight at this early stage of development of the interrelationship of all the different aspects – for example, children with poor fine motor skills who lack confidence and motivation in writing because handwriting is a difficult and unrewarding activity for them, or children who rarely engage in mark-making activities because they have no sense of the place of writing in the adult world.

# Observing early writing

It was stated earlier that observation is central to the assessment of early writing, and the following examples demonstrate this. The first, which took place in a reception class, records a child's engagement with a significant piece of writing – a retelling of a traditional tale. The second records a more typical brief episode in more detail. The third is not a narrative observation; instead, it uses the event sampling method to record two children's engagement in mark-making.

## OBSERVATION

Observation 1: Rosie, 5:2 years

During a period of child-initiated activity, Rosie decided to write the story of the 'Three Little Pigs'. She chose to use paint for her illustrations, and then added writing below and sometimes also above each picture. She produced 13 pages of the story in all over the course of three days, spending over an hour each day on the project. Each page also had her name, and all but the first had a speech bubble. The writing consisted mainly of captions ('This is the mam pig', 'This is a wulf'), but also a traditional story opening and ending ('Once a pona time theai livd three litte pigs'; 'Theai livd happly eva afta'). Rosie wrote without any support, but could be seen sometimes mouthing the words she was writing or segmenting aloud to support her encoding.

## COMMENTARY

Using the framework seen earlier, this observation provides good evidence of Rosie's attitude to writing. It is an activity she chose to engage in and she sustained her interest over considerable lengths of time. She showed understanding of the purpose and form of the story, including both illustration and text, and making the writing more engaging by the use of speech bubbles. She showed awareness of traditional story language, and it may be that she was aware that such stories are retold by different authors. She remembered the characters and the sequence of events in the story, although she did not fully describe all the events – for example, she introduced the men carrying straw, sticks and bricks who asked if the pigs would like the materials, but did not explicitly say that they built houses with them. It was also clear that she could produce phonemically plausible spellings, such as 'bloaing' and 'careeing'.

## OBSERVATION

Observation 2: Tomasz

Tomasz (4:10 years) entered the office role-play area and sat at the desk. He selected a 'to do list' proforma, which was lined with the numbers 1-20 down the left-hand side. He tore it off the pad carefully. He chose a black ballpoint pen, which he held in his right hand with a dynamic tripod grasp. He drew one small square shape next to the number one, two shapes on the line next to the number two, and so on up to 18, where he drew 8 shapes, adding a dot in the centre of each. Towards the end, the shapes were circles rather than squares, and he drew 15 shapes on the 14th line and only 15 on the 17th line. The shapes were all the same size, fitting between the lines, and spaced so they were close together without overlapping. He then drew a row of circles below the last line, and below that a multiplication symbol, two addition symbols and an equals symbol. Tomasz next wrote the numbers 1-11 at the top of the sheet, reversing 4, 5 and 6. He then chose a silver pen and on a separate piece of paper wrote the words dog, wking (working), in, sse (see) and wiv, cutting each one out after writing it. He used a glue stick to stick them down the right-hand side of his to do list. He put the list in his book bag to take home. Tomasz spent 40 minutes in this activity.

## COMMENTARY

This observation showed that Tomasz was interested in mark-making and engaged in the activity independently for a significant length of time; also, what he produced was important to him. It suggests that he was familiar with a range of written symbols, including both letters and numbers, and that he could use his phonic skills to segment words and represent most or all of the phonemes appropriately. It also suggests that he gave meaning to his mark-making – for example, he interpreted the list numbers as a mathematical task and responded accordingly. The observation also showed that he had a good pencil grip and pencil control.

## OBSERVATION

Observation 3: event sampling (notes made each time the child engaged in mark-making)

| Clara | Monika |
|---|---|
| 9.10-9.25 in mark-making area, making maps with another child<br>11.25-11.35 painting at easel<br>1.15-1.20 writing on outdoor chalkboard<br>2.00-2.10 drawing and writing on interactive whiteboard | 2.15-2.20 Making marks on clipboard in outdoor role-play area |

These observations suggest that one child, Clara, engages in a range of mark-making opportunities, using different resources in different provision areas. The other child, Monika, does engage with mark-making, but not as frequently.

It is important to monitor in this way, as some children may never engage in mark-making unless adults require them to do so, and this is something that would need to be addressed, probably by the following strategies.

## IN THE CLASSROOM

- Build opportunities for mark-making into every area of provision, both indoors and outdoors – e.g. clipboards and paper in the construction area, so that children can design or record their constructions; small blank signs for small world play; paper for recording compositions in the music area (see Chapter 11 for an example).

- Provide an interesting variety of materials and mark-making implements, such as small blank books, envelopes, forms to fill in. Ensure that there are safe places to store work in progress, accessible to the children, and that children are aware that they can return to a project over the course of days, rather than needing to complete it in one session.

- Model writing regularly and show children how it forms a part of the adult world, explaining its purpose and nature.

- Show interest in children's mark-making and make it clear that it is valued – for example, by talking to them about it and displaying it.

# The Early Years Foundation Stage Profile

The future of the Early Years Foundation Stage Profile is uncertain; the Department of Education's intention was to replace it with baseline assessment, to be carried out at the beginning of the reception year, but following a pilot this change was not implemented and the Profile remained in place. However, draft revised Early Learning Goals, including those for literacy, were introduced in June 2018, and these were to be piloted, along with a new baseline measure, to be introduced from 2020. The Early Learning Goal for writing states that:

> *Children use their phonic knowledge to write words in ways which match their spoken sounds. They also write some irregular common words. They write simple sentences which can be read by themselves and others. Some words are spelt correctly and others are phonetically plausible.*

> (Standards and Testing Agency, 2017)

The draft Early Learning Goal for writing states that children at the expected level of development will:

- Write recognisable letters, most of which are correctly formed.

- Spell words by identifying sounds in them and representing the sounds with a letter or letters.

- Write simple phrases and sentences that can be read by others.

> (Department for Education, 2018)

It is clear that the goal in both formats focuses on only one aspect of writing – the ability to encode. Children are assessed as meeting the goal (achieving the expected level), not yet meeting the goal (emerging) or exceeding the goal. A best-fit model is used and guidance clearly states that the goal should not be broken down into separate elements that are assessed separately. The description of exceeding also suggests that the emphasis is on encoding.

> *Children can spell phonically regular words of more than 1 syllable as well as many irregular but high frequency words. They use key features of narrative in their own writing.*

(Standards and Testing Agency, 2017)

The reference to features of narrative is welcome, but there is no sense that children at this age may be writing – or indeed perhaps should be writing – in a wide range of forms. However, the exemplification provided by the Standards and Testing Agency (2014) for the expected level of development includes very varied samples: while recounts and stories predominate, there are also lists, letters, instructions, signs and notices, a party invitation, a prescription, posters describing lost animals and toys, and a non-chronological report. The exemplification also usefully shows that there is an expectation that the samples will be child-initiated and often linked to children's interests and preoccupations – experiences inside and outside school, or role play, for example. The Profile Handbook (Standards and Testing Agency, 2017) also makes it clear that assessment should be based on observation and that children should be demonstrating their learning *spontaneously, independently and consistently* (Standards and Testing Agency, 2017, p. 6), and that parents and the children themselves should be contributing to the assessment – an enlightened approach that should perhaps be considered for older children too. Important principles outlined by the Standards and Testing Agency (2017) for this assessment include that the main source of evidence is the practitioner's knowledge of the child, that that knowledge is mainly gathered from observation and interaction with the child, and that good provision allows the child to demonstrate their learning fully.

It can be easy to miss the reference in the physical development Early Learning Goal related to writing.

> *ELG04 Moving and handling: children show good control and coordination in large and small movements. They move confidently in a range of ways, safely negotiating space. They handle equipment and tools confidently, including pencils for writing.*

(Standards and Testing Agency, 2017, p. 30)

The draft Early Learning Goal for Fine Motor Skills is more specific, stating that children at the expected level of development will *Hold a pencil comfortably using the tripod grip* (DfE, 2018).

It is worth noting that of all the many fine motor skills that children may develop, such as cutting with scissors, eating with cutlery, spreading glue or jam, sewing with needles, making Lego models, and indeed using a wide range of mark-making tools such as felt-tip pens, paint brushes and crayons for drawing, using pencils for writing is the only one specified in physical development. It should also be noted that the exemplification materials provide no further guidance as to expectations: confidence perhaps implies a level of skill, but this is not stated.

# Conclusion

A literacy-rich environment and meaningful literacy experiences are likely to promote positive attitudes to writing in young children. Skilful teaching should result in good progress in writing in the Early Years Foundation Stage, but attitudes are crucial: children who are curious about writing and confident about their own ability to write will be motivated to engage with and persist in writing activities. Assessment is the key to planning effective teaching, and in the Foundation Stage this involves very careful consideration of children's mark-making; detailed attention not only to children's knowledge of phoneme–grapheme correspondences, but also, crucially, their ability to hear phonemes in words; and observation of children engaged in writing activities, including their letter formation, but going well beyond this to note evidence of attitude, understanding and behaviours.

# References

Department for Education (DfE) (2018) *Early Years Foundation Stage Profile: 2018 Handbook* (pilot version September 2018). London: Department for Education.

Early Education (2012) *Development Matters in the Early Years Foundation Stage*. London: Early Education (The British Association for Early Childhood Education).

Gentry, JR (1982) An Analysis of Developmental Spelling in GNYS AT WRK. *The Reading Teacher, 36*: 192–200.

Standards and Testing Agency (2014) *EYFS Profile Exemplification for the Level of Learning and Development Expected at the End of the EYFS*. London: Department for Education.

Standards and Testing Agency (2017) *Early Years Foundation Stage Profile: 2018 Handbook*. London: Department for Education.

# 3
# FICTION

┌─────────────── IN THIS CHAPTER ───────────────┐

This chapter considers how children's story writing develops, and how their mastery of the key elements of stories - plot, character, setting, atmosphere, language effects - can be assessed. Some of the common difficulties of fiction writing will be discussed, and for each sample analysed there will be suggestions of next steps for the writer.

└────────────────────────────────────────────────┘

Children write stories regularly during their primary years, although many of them will then write few or none during the rest of their education and the rest of their lives. Many children love writing stories and draw effectively on their reading of fiction during the process. However, for some children writing successful fiction is much more difficult than writing non-fiction: they find it difficult to orchestrate those different elements that make stories successful. Constructing a plot in which interesting or even exciting things happen and everything is neatly resolved at the end is not easy. Cain and Oakhill (1996) emphasised the importance in stories of a series of causally related events, and suggested that reading comprehension skills affected children's ability to produce coherent stories. Traditionally, children have been supported in this aspect of fiction writing by opportunities to retell known stories, but these may be too complicated for the younger writer, so need to be carefully chosen if they are to work as a bridge towards children constructing their own plots. In recent years, the Talk for Writing initiative, first introduced in 2008 (Talk4Writing, n.d.), introduced a process in which children first learned and orally retold stories, then changed elements while keeping the basic structure of the story, then invented their own stories. The three stages are known as *imitate, innovate, invent*. The approach was developed because of a concern that many children did not have a personal bank of known stories to draw on, in terms of both structure and language, as do children who have had a rich diet of stories from their earliest years.

The key features of simple stories are as follows.

- A structure with an opening introducing main characters and setting.

- A series of events involving complications and probably building up to a crisis.

- A resolution of the problems and an ending.

- First- or third-person narration.

- Use of the past tense (or occasionally the present).

- Language effects to engage the reader – e.g. similes, repetition.

Beyond these generic features, much fiction belongs to recognisable genres such as historical fiction, fables, myths or science fiction, and each of these has its own characteristic features. As story writing becomes more sophisticated, the writer may choose to omit a traditional introduction and leave readers to work out for themselves who the characters are, where and when the story is happening, and what led up to the first event which is narrated. The writer might also choose to write in the present tense, or to write in a very simple, unadorned style, or to use more than one narrator.

Progression in story writing is likely to be evidenced by a greater understanding of how to capture and keep the attention of the reader, greater skill in writing in a range of genres and increased control of different language effects. Note that in the next steps discussed for each writer whose work is considered in this chapter, the focus is on next steps in narrative writing only. It is easy to be distracted by punctuation, sentence structure and so on, and to forget that these are stories, and the first and main response to them should be whether they succeed as stories. Are we hooked in at the very beginning? Do we want to keep reading to find out what happens next? Does the ending provide a satisfying resolution? Does the story have any confusing points where we are not quite sure what is happening? Are there any loose ends that should have been tied up? Do we have some sense of the characters and setting? Does the language used enhance the story?

In the early stages of writing development, children write only a sentence or two, but some of these sentences can be categorised as embryonic stories because something happens. Often when children have started by drawing a picture, the text is simply a description of the picture: the following examples, all produced by the same child over the course of a year, are a mixture of description and narrative (note that support was given with spellings).

## CHILDREN'S WRITING

Jessica, reception: picture captions

Here is my doll.

There is a field with lots of trees in.

Here is mummy and daddy duck.

Here are my pancakes in the oven.

My sisters are playing with me.

The weathervane fell off the church.

Here is my cat he is going to have his food.

Here is the leopard in the jungle.

Is the fox running after the rabbit yes it is.

Marta is throwing the ball and the spaceship is going up.

He has gone off on his trip already with his quilt.

Here is the mouse he is trying to open the door.

Here is a policeman looking down some stairs.

The king is coming out of the castle to smell the flowers.

Here is a caterpillar he is looking for worms to eat.

Here is a frog spouting all the water out when he laughed.

The giant ate ten children.

## COMMENTARY

The samples show an impressive range in terms of subject matter, including simple domestic situations, but also more exciting scenarios, such as the spaceship setting off, and a number of animal characters and characters from fairy tales (the king and the giant). At the beginning of the year, captions tended simply to label what was in the picture, and there were examples of this throughout the year. These could be seen as consisting of one or more element of a story – either setting (a field with lots of trees) or characters (mummy and daddy duck), but over time more captions included events, some in the past (The weathervane fell off the church), some in the present (the fox running after the rabbit) and even the future (he is going to have his food). Some of the events suggest a problem (the mouse trying to open the door, the caterpillar looking for worms) and therefore seem incomplete, while 'The giant ate ten children' could be seen as a complete story. The frog story is probably a brief partial retelling of the traditional story of Tiddalik.

### *Next steps for Jessica*

While Jessica was happy to draw and to add a caption to her drawing, she showed no inclination to write at greater length as the year went by. For her, the writing was simply a summary of everything she had put into her drawing, and an adult requirement the purpose of which she did not fully understand. To support her in developing her stories, an adult response of interest and a desire to know more and to prompt her to give more information would probably be the most successful approach: questions such as 'Did the fox catch the rabbit in your story?' or 'And what did the policeman see at the bottom of the stairs?' would suggest to Jessica that her audience is keen to know more, and that a picture cannot tell a story in the way that writing can. It is important that children see that there is a point in writing at greater length, and that is to do with how much we communicate, not how much paper we fill. Shared writing provides valuable opportunities to model all the important aspects of story writing for early writers – considering the audience for the story, making decisions about character, setting and plot, and orally drafting sentences before writing them down. The provision of small blank books can also encourage children to make their stories longer.

The following two examples show children drawing successfully on stories they may have known for years: on the whole, story models will need to be simpler than stories that children are reading or hearing if they are to work well. Dylan's story is based on Judith Kerr's classic *The Tiger Who Came to Tea* (1968), while Liam uses John Burningham's *Mr Gumpy's Motor Car* (1973); it is worth noting that Burningham himself had used this story structure before in *Mr Gumpy's Outing* (1970).

## CHILDREN'S WRITING

Dylan, year 1: The loin who came to lunch

wons there was a little boy then there was a nock at the door Drew opend the door therer was a big, fury, loin exyoosme but can I have lunch whith you I am verry hugry of cors come in the loin eat all the Burgus! and pizza! and Brock the TV then Brock the wiiii thank you I think I better go now! and he eat the mackaronechez! and the garlickbred.

## CHILDREN'S WRITING

Liam, year 2: Mr Gumpy's day trip to York

Mr Gumpy woke up he thought he would like to go to York. So he got dressed up and had his breakfast. He went to the car and went drive he saw the children the, rabbit the, cat the, dog the, pig, the chikens the, calf and the goat asked can they go. Yes said Mr Gumpy but it will be a squash so they went in the car a drove. Then they saw the castle musimen so they parked and went inside. When they saw the castle musimen they went outside but when they went the river taken all the animals and children and iven Mr Gumpy! it was raing so much and they where somewhere they didien't know the place but then they saw there car and drove back home as cwick as they could. Mr Gumpy said we might have time to swim then Mr Gumpy said good by have a nother trip with me!

# COMMENTARY

Dylan's story sticks fairly closely to the original, changing the main characters and updating some details. He does not include an ending to match the one in the original story, which involves the family going out to eat as the tiger has eaten all their food. He does add a detail – the breaking of the television and the Wii – which is not present in the original, and suggests a more anti-social, or at least clumsy, character. Dylan includes direct speech, using language drawn from the original. Liam uses his model more flexibly: rather than having the passengers embark one by one, with permission from Mr Gumpy, he gives much more attention to the outing, where there is a sequence of events which Liam has invented. The characters are carried away by the river, an echo perhaps of the earlier Mr Gumpy story where a boat overturns and all the characters fall in the river. In Liam's version, they manage to find the car and the ending returns to the model, again using wording from the original. Liam has taken a very simple cumulative story and elaborated the plot quite significantly. Although not every detail is clear (Had the river flooded? How did the characters get back to the car park?), Liam has shown the confidence to make the story his own.

## Next steps for Dylan and Liam

The Talk for Writing approach is flexible enough that it can provide differentiated support for children: some may stick fairly closely to the model, while others are much keener and more confident to innovate. The ultimate goal, however, is to invent new stories. However, having knowledge of basic story structures can be helpful in this. Lewis (1999) suggested that structuring stories was difficult for children, and her project identified a number of basic structures that could be found in many children's stories; these included journey stories, problem and resolution stories, cumulative and reverse cumulative stories, and days of the week stories. In the project, children were first immersed in stories with the same structure, then discussed and recorded the structure through drawing, and finally used it as a basis for their own story. Once children have this repertoire of basic structures, they can select from them and adapt them as they choose, and will continue to recognise them in stories they read – noticing, too, that many stories contain elements of more than one structure. This explicit focus on structure would be helpful for Dylan and Liam. However, children who have been exposed to many stories in their early years are likely to draw on these quite naturally in their own fiction writing, as the following example demonstrates.

---

## CHILDREN'S WRITING

Ana, year 1: The magic door

Once upon a time therer was a little girl called Ana. She allways wanted to go on an adventure. One day she found a rondom old door just silting there Ana steped inside all there was is the othor side of her bedroom. she stept in it and the adventure began. In the door was the most dark and goomest forest Ana had ever seen. she had a wonder arownd until she was lost ohno Ana said im holst I need to get home she sow a creature she took a photo then there was more oh she

*(Continued)*

---

(Continued)

said hello little guy she said now I need to find a way home she thout then she found a cave she went inside it was dark it is good she had a torch she turnd it on and she chouod see a huge bear! runnnnn!!! she shoulted she ran as fast as she chould the bear was catching up and she chould see the door she leped in and locked the door phew Ana said I am never going there again she said. The end.

## COMMENTARY

This is a long and impressive story for a child of this age. The beginning, with the magic door and the forest, is reminiscent of CS Lewis's *The Lion, the Witch and the Wardrobe* (1950), although it is a little surprising that Ana would know this story, and possibly also Maurice Sendak's *Where the Wild Things Are* (1963). The ending appears to draw on Michael Rosen's *We're Going on a Bear Hunt* (1989). Ana has successfully integrated these different sources into her story, and her language also reflects her knowledge of stories – 'the adventure began', 'the most dark and goomest forest Ana had ever seen'. While there are one or two loose ends in the story – why did she go into the cave when she was looking for the way home? how did she find the way home while being chased by the bear? – the story rattles along so energetically that the reader is hardly aware of these. Character is indicated briefly (She always wanted to go on an adventure), though it is not clear what the creatures Ana meets first are. The setting is also presented economically but effectively in her description of the forest. Ana makes good use of direct speech, in particular the main character talking to herself ('Now I need to find a way home,' 'Runnn!!!' 'Phew I am never going there again.') This story is discussed in terms of its punctuation in Chapter 8.

### *Next steps for Ana*

Ana needs to continue to develop her awareness of the needs of her audience. Working with a writing partner would be very helpful here, with a list of prompts to support discussion and feedback. It is important that children become used to discussing their writing with others from early on, and this can be modelled by the teacher in whole-class teaching, with guided writing sessions allowing children to develop the relevant skills with support.

## IN THE CLASSROOM

Prompts to support evaluation or redrafting might include the following.

- What did you particularly like about the writing?
- Were there any bits of the writing you did not understand completely?

- Were there any parts where you would have liked to know more?
- Did anything puzzle you about the writing?

Of course we would probably not ask a child of this age to redraft the writing; simply discussing possible changes helps her to begin to see her own writing through a reader's eye. Older writers may also have difficulty in doing this; their stories may be very clear in their own heads, but are not fully captured on paper. This may be a particular issue when they are drawing on a source such as a film, as can be seen in the next example, which is perhaps influenced by the musical *Little Shop of Horrors*, or a similar fantasy.

## CHILDREN'S WRITING

Mariette, year 3: Story

"HI! I'm Rose." "I look after my Mum's plant shop when she's away." A few days ago things were going missig in the plant shop and the plants seem to be getting bigger twice a day! "I'm going to find out what's happing the plant shop" "I'm going in."

Everything is gigantic. "Uh oh! The plants! There walking around with there roots and there grabbing seeds with there leves! Thie've got plant pots on there flower heads. It's hallareeus" "I think I'm going behind the counter. If I can get through." "Hey" said a plant. "What" I replied. "Why are you here?" arnsward the plant. "I own the shop" "Hey! Wait a minite you're a plant" "Ahh" I interrupted "Get away from my shop." "Wait! I'm good, all I want here is to get out." "But I don't know how to?" shouted the plant. "What's happening here?" I asked. "I belive the Quween (vilot) is hungry and wants food!" Arnsward, the plant. changing the subject I delitfully asked "What's your name" I wanted a reply but I didn't get one. Then I said "my name is Rose!! "Right I rember the antidote but first we need some uncon bulibs" said the plant. "I know where we can find them" I replied. I got them from the counter. We fed them to the plants then everything was back to normal.

## COMMENTARY

Mariette sets up the problem in the story quickly and develops it with relevant detail as Rose enters the shop. However, the plot does not then develop into a crisis, turning instead into somewhat confused dialogue. The resolution is brief and anti-climactic, suggesting perhaps that Mariette ran out of time or interest. The story needs a better balance between narrative and speech; this lack of balance sometimes results when children have encountered the story they are drawing on as a film or play, where the setting and action are seen rather than described and the dialogue is foregrounded. Mariette's dialogue generally moves the action forward, but at some points it is not clear who is speaking. If a reporting clause is not used, it ought to be possible to infer without any difficulty who the speaker is. (Mariette's choice of verbs in the reporting clauses is discussed in Chapter 7.)

## Next steps for Mariette

Mariette needs to balance the elements of stories – description, action and dialogue. To help her to see the need for this, she could first highlight all the direct speech in her story and consider which parts could be converted to action or description. For example, the sight that greets Rose as she goes into the shop could be conveyed as a simple description. Mariette also needs to ensure that it is always clear who is speaking. A response partner could point out where she needs to add a reporting clause to achieve this, and starting on a new line for each new speaker would also help. It is important that children do not feel that they must always use a reporting clause, but if one is not used the writer should check that readers can work out who the speaker is, either because two speakers are alternating or because the meaning of what is said makes this clear.

Some writing combines elements of more than one text type – for example, fictionalised accounts of historical events. In the following sample, the class has been studying Ancient Egypt in history and heard the story of Cleopatra. The plot is therefore given, but the writer needed to dramatise it and engage his readers even though the story might be familiar to them.

---

## CHILDREN'S WRITING

Misha, year 4: Retelling of an Ancient Egyptian event

On the darck brown ship, in the middle of the sweltering, wavy sea it was meltingly hot. Queen Cleopatra was watching her war ships be defeated and destroyed. She could hear the loud bubbuling and gurguling of war ships sinking. The rusty ships were being destroyed by garstly Romans coming to invad Egypt.

"Retreat Captin Retrit! They will sink us or capture us to execut. The petrefied Captin immidiatly told his sailors to turn the ship and retreat to the shore. He completly agreed with Cleopatra and wanted to save himself. Cleopatra's slaves comforted her with henkachine and sweet wine.

Terrified and screaming, they arrived on the darck and brown shorses of Egypt. Standing nearby was Cleopatra's golden charoiet and armoed horses she jumped on quickly and cracked her whip in the air to start her horses off. Scared as she bumped over rocks and slide throughe sand she made her horses go quikly. When she got there she ran through the room opening doors as she went. Her footsteps rattled loudly through the stone chambers.

When she got to her bedroom she ran straight for a small woven basket. Inside was a green, spine-chilling asp. Cleopatra thought; then she pulled the asps tail around and threw the asp and made it crash it's head on the bloody wall the asp slitherd back, Cleopatra trembuled and picked up the asp and strecht it, the asp got so angry that the asp bit Cleopatra in her chest.

---

## COMMENTARY

This is a vivid and compelling account. Misha includes many telling details that bring the story to life most effectively. The heat is conveyed through his word choices in the first sentence, 'sweltering' and 'meltingly hot'. The situation is conveyed economically – a battle at sea, defeat for the Egyptians, imminent Roman invasion. The 'bubbling and gurgling' of the sinking ships is an unexpected and well-chosen detail. Direct speech conveys the urgency of the moment and Cleopatra's leadership. Her state of mind is suggested by the slaves 'comforting' her. The pace is kept up as Cleopatra reaches land and races for her palace; again, the details of the golden chariot and armoured horses create a vivid picture. The picture of Cleopatra running through the palace is equally strong; the reader sees the series of rooms and doors and hears the clatter of the feet. The last scene is quite horrifying in its violence, but this is purposeful and not excessive. Only in the last sentence does the impact of the writing lessen, and it is disappointing that the writer has not completed the story.

## Next steps for Misha

Children are encouraged to focus on story openings, considering how to hook the reader in, how to introduce setting and characters effectively, and how to lead in to the problem which will start the plot moving forward. Misha would benefit from a similar emphasis on story endings – how to draw together threads of the plot and ensure that a resolution is reached, and how to produce a sense of completion. As always, reading will offer many solutions: children's stories end often with a meal, or a comment from a character or even from the narrator, or the drawing of a moral, or even a look to the future. Discussion of these endings and of ways of producing a satisfying ending is important. Can there be a link back to the introduction? Is the 'it was all a dream?' acceptable or simply an irritating cheat? For more sophisticated writers, a flashback structure frames the main story with an introduction and conclusion which are set in the present. Of course, it is unlikely that a whole class of children will be able to time their story writing so exactly that they all finish together, but it can be useful to give them indications of how much time they have so that the ending is not omitted or rushed. They might also be encouraged to finish unfinished stories in additional time or at home.

In order to focus on specific aspects of fiction writing, children are often asked to write a character or setting description. This can be a useful strategy, although they will then need to move on to integrating their descriptions into stories, where often details of character, place or time are scattered through the writing rather than forming a chunk at the beginning. There can also be an issue when children spend too long on setting and character before the story really gets going; as school children are essentially writing short stories, there simply is not time for this. The short story format requires economy – every detail must count, with character and setting sketched out in a few strokes, and the plot must be relatively simple. In the next two samples, children have been asked to focus on one element only: Jemima describes a character and Zoe a setting.

## COMMENTARY

The following description combines details of the character's appearance, his personality and hints about his past. We are told about his stature, but all the other information about his appearance

---

## CHILDREN'S WRITING

Jemima, year 5: Character description

*The man on the ship had reflective goggles that were strapped on tightly. His buttened waistcoat was illuminous and his scarf was silky and was wrapped tightly over his mouth so not a noise came out of him. He was strange and mysterious and had many secrets he would not tell. Also, he wore buckled boots and mactching navy trousers. He looked deadly on the outside but had a kind and caring heart on the inside. He was towering and slender but brave and adventurous and always determined. Who was this person you say? ... He was an aircraft pilot. He looked obnoxious so that's why he covererd his revolting face. Also his eyes showed neglected and his heart seemed like nobody loved him anymore.*

---

relates to his clothing; towards the end of the description we discover the reason for this, as his face is hidden by his goggles and scarf. It is not clear why his face is 'revolting'; the rest of the passage would suggest an explanation such as injuries caused by a flying accident, rather than this being his natural appearance. The two adjectives chosen give a slightly jarring note here, and a more thoughtful vocabulary choice such as 'disfigured', 'damaged' or 'scarred' might have worked better. It may be that the intention is to return to this in the narrative. Details about the clothing reinforce the suggestion that it is used for concealment – both goggles and scarf are fastened 'tightly' so there is no danger of accidentally revealing the face – or even allowing him to speak. The threatening appearance is, however, contrasted with his essential nature – the 'kind and caring heart'. There is a slightly less successful contrast between his build and his personality – 'towering and slender but brave and adventurous'. It could be that the word 'slender' is intended to suggest a physical fragility, which the rest of the sentence then contradicts in terms of his nature; this would repeat the outside/inside comparison of the previous sentence. Two sentences very successfully convey hints of a difficult life: the last one, which very much engages the reader on the side of this quite tragic character, and the delightful 'He was strange and mysterious and had many secrets he would not tell'. This is a simple sentence in its construction which powerfully suggests that the character is not like others and that his life is complex and troubled; the use of 'would' rather than 'could' implies that the secrecy is part of his nature rather than simply a necessity forced on him by circumstances. Again, there is a neat reflection of his concealment of his physical appearance. This is an example of what Loane (2017) describes as a 'thesis statement' – a sentence which sums up the character, giving a characteristic which will be a key to the events of the story. By the end of the paragraph the reader very much wants to know more about the character and his past. The authorial interjection – 'Who was this person you say? He was an aircraft pilot.' – gives away very little really; the narrator's apparent openness and helpfulness is not borne out by the information given.

### *Next steps for Jemima*

Jemima is a skilful creator of character. Discussion of her word picture of the aviator would help her to consider if there are any details that do not add anything useful to the description, and whether her writing has the effect she intended. She might also analyse her own character descriptions and those of other writers to see how different elements work together – for example, physical appearance is often treated as a reflection or indication of personality. In completing her story, she would need to make sure that the hints dropped in this passage are picked up in the narrative, so that readers do eventually discover the answers to the questions raised here.

## CHILDREN'S WRITING

Zoe, year 5: Setting description

Harry took a step forward and froze, along the path hee saw silver blood shineing along the winding path, the horizon was a wall of gloomy mist, so gloomy all you could see was yourself.

He looked up and crouched and looked at the spider like path he saw a monsturus and spicky bush. Then out of knw were a deid snake came up to harry in pain, Harry took a step and froze, infront of him was lot's of werewolfs trying to attack him, as well as skull evil shaped trees with Red EYES! And this time the mist was as gloomy as coal! so all you could see was these mysterious red *detes* floating in midair.

## COMMENTARY

Children often enjoy horror story writing, drawing on their experience of film, but this is a form in which less can be more; throwing in all the elements does not necessarily result in successful stories. Zoe's setting references blood, spiders, snakes, werewolves and skulls in quick succession, with limited impact on the reader. More effective is her inclusion of the mist: she begins by describing it as a wall, which works because we know it cannot be a physical boundary but can imagine how solid it looked. She uses the word 'gloomy' three times, which might be because she cannot think of an alternative or has not noticed that she has repeated it, but repetition can be effective; here the choice works well because of the dual meaning of the word – dark colour or dark mood. This image contrasts well with the image of the trail of blood, which is 'silvery' and 'shining' – again, simple but unexpected and effective word choices.

### Next steps for Zoe

Zoe needs to consider how to build up her descriptions more gradually, choosing details to focus on carefully. She would benefit from reading examples of the genre, and seeing such writing being modelled by her teacher. In writing settings for other types of story Zoe might find it helpful to work from first-hand experience, so that she learns to notice significant details about a place, including perhaps sounds and smells as well as what she can see. Pictures can also be a useful support, rather than expecting the young writer to create a setting in the mind or recall one.

# Working in different genres

A challenge for the developing writer is to write in a genre such as the horror story, as we have just seen, or the historical story, as we saw with the Cleopatra story. There is still a need to construct a good plot and engage the reader, but the writer also needs to recognise what is distinctive about the genre and include those distinctive features. These can be simple – for example, avoiding inappropriate details such as a gun in a myth – or more difficult to achieve, such as style. Some children are able to do this quite easily once they have read some examples, rather as some people can adopt different accents at will; others find it much more problematic to imitate a genre. The following example shows a child writing in the style of Rudyard Kipling's *Just So Stories* (1902), of which the best known is probably *How the Elephant got his Trunk*. It is likely that George has experience of the CBeebies Tinga Tinga Tales cartoon adaptation of the story, since he replicates its ending.

## CHILDREN'S WRITING

George, year 4: Why Rhino has a horn

We all know that Rhino is the owner of a magnificent horn, but did you know that there was a time when Rhino didn't have a horn and didn't charge. He looked rather like a big fat grey cow …

One very hot day, Rhino went to the watering hole to have a drink. Earlyer that day us monkeys put glue on Rhino's head. Then Rhino suddenly saw that at the bottom of the water there was a pile of bones. This very big curved bone stuck onto his head! All of the animals tried and tried to pull the bone off, but they couldn't. It was stuck!

"Hey Rhino you don't look like a cow anymore!" shouted Giarffe from a mile away. "Watch this, as well!" Rhino shouted back. Then Rhino charged at a tree, consequently, the tree fell down! So there you are, that's how Rhino got his horn and why I have a long tail, that's a whole other story.

## COMMENTARY

Kipling's stories share a number of features.

*   An explanation of a feature of an animal's appearance – the camel's hump, the leopard's spots.

*   Addressing the reader directly ('O Best Beloved').

*   Direct speech, including by animals.

*   Characters with animal names only (the Giraffe, the Zebra).

*   Language typical of a writer of the period, writing for children.

George has provided an explanation of how the Rhino got his horn, and his final sentence suggests that this story is one of a series, as with the *Just So* Stories. His introduction is reminiscent of the opening of *The Elephant's Child*, describing the appearance of the animal in question in the long ago time when it did not have its distinctive feature. However, George makes another animal in the story, a monkey, the narrator, rather than maintaining Kipling's authorial voice. He includes direct speech from the animals, and some of his language has a feel of another age ('a magnificent horn', 'He looked rather like … ', 'So there you are … '), but this is not consistently maintained, with phrases such as 'us monkeys' and 'Hey Rhino' sounding rather more modern. However, this is a good attempt at a story of this kind, bearing in mind that George is unlikely to have heard the stories read aloud many times or to have read them for himself.

## Next steps for George

George has shown himself able to incorporate the features of a particular type of story into his own writing, while still producing a successful plot. Continuing to experiment with different genres will provide challenge and will broaden his knowledge of fiction.

He may also enjoy subverting or playing about with genres – for example, writing in the style of a traditional tale but with the story set in the present day.

George's use of punctuation is discussed in Chapter 8.

# Conclusion

The chapter began by noting the prevalence of fiction writing in the primary school, compared with later phases of education and adult life. Fiction and poetry writing used to be seen almost as arts that could not be taught, relying instead on a creative nature and inspiration. More recently, such writing has been seen as a craft that can be taught, as the popularity of creative writing courses in universities and writing groups shows. In primary schools, it has been recognised that children often need far more direct teaching than was thought in the past if they are to become successful story writers. The model of reading widely to immerse oneself in the genre, analysing examples to see 'how they work', trying out a first draft and then redrafting and being given feedback, allows children to learn and practise the skills of the craft. It is important that assessment of stories, and the feedback given to children, focuses on the elements that make fiction successful – is the reader hooked in quickly? Does the writer create an atmosphere or mood appropriate to the type of story? Is the plot well constructed? Does the story read well? Elements such as paragraphing or sentence structure should only be considered in relation to how they make the story a better story. For example, paragraphing is appropriate in longer stories, but not if it means that each paragraph is only two or three sentences long, and it should reflect the division of the story into clear scenes or sections of the plot. For many children, story writing is a pleasurable experience, an opportunity to use their imagination and creativity, and it is important to maintain that sense of enjoyment, rather than constraining it with a list of somewhat arbitrary success criteria.

# References

Burningham, J (1970) *Mr Gumpy's Outing*. London: Cape.

Burningham, J (1973) *Mr Gumpy's Motor Car*. London: Cape.

Cain, K and Oakhill, J (1996) The nature of the relationship between comprehension skill and the ability to tell a story. *British Journal of Developmental Psychology*, *14*: 187–201.

Kerr, J (1968) *The Tiger Who Came to Tea*. London: HarperCollins.

Kipling, R (1902) *Just So Stories For Little Children*. London: Macmillan.

Lewis, CS (1950) *The Lion, The Witch and the Wardrobe*. London: Geoffrey Bles.

Lewis, M (1999) Developing Children's Narrative Writing using Story Structures. In Goodwin, P (ed.) *The Literate Classroom*. London: David Fulton.

Loane, G (2017) *Developing Young Writers in the Classroom: I've got something to say*. Abingdon: Routledge.

Rosen, M (1989) *We're Going on a Bear Hunt*. New York: Margaret K McElderry Books.

Sendak, M (1963) *Where the Wild Things Are*. New York: Harper & Row.

Talk for Writing (n.d.) Available at: www.talk4writing.co.uk/ (accessed 6 April 2018).

# 4
# NON-FICTION WRITING

— IN THIS CHAPTER —

This chapter explores the subject knowledge specific to non-fiction writing and the assessment of children's writing of this text type. It outlines the essential elements of different types of non-fiction writing and how children can develop specific writing skills.

In children's non-fiction writing we are looking for their ability to select appropriate information, organise it effectively and communicate it clearly. These skills are likely to be important for them throughout their education and for some in their careers. They run alongside the ability to evaluate information – is it true? is it relevant? is it important? – which is a critical skill useful in many aspects of life. As with any writing, children also need to be able to engage their readers and anticipate how much knowledge of the subject they are likely to have, and what they might want or need to know. Some of those more generic writing skills are dealt with in other chapters; this chapter will focus particularly on the selection and organisation of information, and children's ability to write in a form that is appropriate for the purpose of the writing. Selection of information is a key aspect of successful non-fiction writing, and the process of writing depends on the process of information gathering. This can make non-fiction writing a complex task; while teachers may at times give support with both the selection of information and its organisation, it is important that children learn to manage and integrate the two aspects independently.

Bearne (2002) suggests that discussion of non-fiction text in many classrooms tends to focus on presentational features – headings, indexes, captions, bullet points and so on – rather than on how ideas and information are organised, and that this then causes difficulties when children are asked to gather information and use it in their own writing. Surface features should reflect deep structure rather than replace it. Over the last two decades or so, the use of writing frames, proposed by Lewis and Wray (1998) to support children in structuring their writing, has become widespread. Writing frames provide children with a framework of sections or sentence starters, meaning that often the organising and structuring of content has effectively been done for them; a similar approach is the provision of subheadings by the teacher. This removes the challenge, but also the creativity and pleasure of shaping the text independently, and it is important that children should learn to do this for themselves: writing frames, as Lewis and Wray pointed out, should be a temporary crutch, not a permanent support.

# Text types

Arnold (1999) suggests that texts organised chronologically, whether fiction or non-fiction, are easier to produce than those that are organised hierarchically into categories and subcategories, such as a text on the Romans, which might include information on the army, what Romans ate and Roman towns – and the town section might include a subsection on Roman houses, with a subsection within that on how houses were heated. While it is important to remember that the classification of non-fiction texts into different categories is somewhat artificial, and that many texts have features of more than one genre, however they are classified, it is probably helpful for young writers to have some sense of different text types with different purposes and different forms. It also helps them to see what forms such as accounts of historical events, biographies and autobiographies, and diaries have in common – that they are all narratives. Many schools still make use of the approach of the National Literacy Strategy (1998) which proposed six main text types:

- recounts
- instructions
- non-chronological reports
- explanations
- persuasive writing
- discussions.

Bearne and Reedy (2018) outline the same basic types, adding evaluation to include forms such as book and film reviews, and sports reports. The Talk for Writing approach (Corbett and Strong, 2011) uses these text types, but not the term 'non-chronological report', preferring instead 'information writing', as this was used by the National Strategies in secondary schools. The National Strategies progression papers (n.d.) provide useful guidance on the distinctive features of different text types, including fiction, and what progression in each might look like.

The samples to be considered in this chapter will include examples of these text types, while recognising that children will also be asked to write non-fiction texts that do not fit neatly into these categories, and that it is important that they should do this. Children often spontaneously write in a range of forms that they have not been taught but have encountered: this is shown clearly in a number of child-initiated samples by a five-year-old child after one term in reception.

## COMMENTARY

Maria shows that she is able to understand the purpose of texts she encounters and includes some of their features in her own writing. The shopping list is laid out in list format; the information

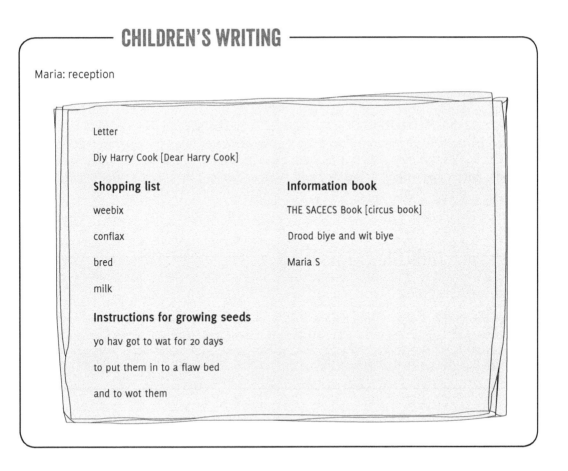

CHILDREN'S WRITING

Maria: reception

Letter

Diy Harry Cook [Dear Harry Cook]

**Shopping list**

weebix

conflax

bred

milk

**Instructions for growing seeds**

yo hav got to wat for 20 days

to put them in to a flaw bed

and to wot them

**Information book**

THE SACECS Book [circus book]

Drood biye and wit biye

Maria S

book cover gives the title and her own name as author and illustrator. She lists three instructions for growing seeds, although these are not in the right order. It is more important to note that she demonstrates the interest and confidence to attempt these different forms, and that already she sees writing as a purposeful activity, embedded in the real world.

### Next steps for Maria

At this stage, Maria needs adults to continue to share with her a wide range of texts, talking about their purposes and forms. Adults also need to show interest in her writing, discussing it with her and acknowledging her intention and achievement. She could be encouraged to continue with incomplete pieces, such as the letter and the book, but this should not be forced if she has lost interest.

## Recounts

The main features of recounts, which are probably the commonest non-fiction text type written by children in school, are usually:

- a structure consisting of an introduction to the participants and main event, events recounted in chronological order, and a conclusion that summarises or comments on the events;

- language features including the past tense, adverbials of time and often a focus on the participants in the events.

Recounts need to include key events, but are often more successful when they also include incidents which are particularly interesting or amusing, and details which bring the recount to life. Because they are telling a story, they may have much in common with fiction, and writers may be trying to create atmosphere and tension in their recounts, or using humour, in order to engage their readers.

Two recounts will be analysed, looking for these features.

## CHILDREN'S WRITING

Lucas, year 1: Diary entry

First I got on the bampy, bright coach and we went then we went inside. Next I saw Oley the Bexlpuse I had 2 2ps and it said ... I am Oley We saw fish, crocadels, snakes, meerkats and when a then we ate lunch. we sat down for lunch and then we played on the grass because we had a play at lunch. but then we went. "(I loved it it's fun.")

## COMMENTARY

Lucas has not provided an introduction: the reader does not know who 'I' or 'we' are, and although we can infer that the main event is a school trip, he does not state this or say where they went. This can be one of the difficulties of the diary entry as a format: diaries are intended to be private writing, and therefore there is no need to meet criteria that might be expected of writing for a wider audience than oneself. But a further difficulty in terms of audience is that Lucas knows that anyone who is likely to read his writing (his teacher or classmates) also went on the trip, and therefore has a great deal of prior knowledge to draw on. Lucas has recognised the need for a conclusion by providing a quotation from himself; this appears to be a feature he has noticed in other texts and has independently decided to use here. He recounts six events, which we can assume are in chronological order, and he uses 'first', 'next', 'and then', 'but then' to indicate this. It is worth noting that use of such vocabulary does not necessarily enhance narrative, as the reader will assume that the events are in chronological order unless told otherwise. There is often, however, a great deal of emphasis on this feature in school, perhaps because adverbials of time are easy to spot and easy to model. Lucas writes consistently in the past tense. He tries to include some interesting detail: the use of 'bumpy' and 'bright' to describe the coach suggests that he has been given a reminder about using adjectives before starting to write, but this is not really successful. Younger writers often focus on less important elements in the recount – typically, the bus journey, the toilet visits and lunch rather than the place they are visiting. Lucas also includes the detail about Olly, but does not explain it sufficiently (presumably, it is some sort of slot machine) for the reader to understand why he found this detail worth including. The animals that were, we assume, the main point of the visit, are simply listed without any additional information or comments.

## Next steps for Lucas

Lucas needs to consider what a 'real' audience (in other words, readers who have not been on the trip) would consider the most important and interesting events in the visit. He could have focused on the animals he saw, describing them and what they were doing. He might also have thought about any amusing, exciting or frightening events during the day. Talk is essential in helping children plan what to write about, and they need to imagine they are talking to someone who has not shared the experience with them – or even better, talk to a person who really does want to know about it. Lucas also needs to make sure he includes an introduction to his recounts: answering the questions Who? When? What? will help him to include necessary information.

Moving on to the work of an older writer, we can see that it is important for children to be able to write about events they have not had personal experience of. This type of writing involves researching and gathering information, unlike the recounting of a personal experience; both, of course, involve the selection of what information to include.

## CHILDREN'S WRITING

Emma, year 5: Sinking of the Titanic

This monstrous boat hit this deadly iceburg very early in the moing. This event happened 4 day's into the Titanic maiden voyage. One off the people on the life boat's said they would be back for breakfast; they would fix the damage and everyone would be able to get back on. The closest ship did not do anything to help; they knew it was a ship because they could see the outline (this ship was called Calafornia.)

It took on 400 tons of watre after the collision. It was 2 hours and 40 minutes for this boat to sink. The opeing of the hole was 12 cubic feet. The watch tower gave six warnings.

## COMMENTARY

Emma introduces the recount briefly in her first sentence. She then includes two details that add to the tragedy of the event – the over-optimism of the people on the boat and the *Californian*'s failure to help. Emma moves on to give some statistics about the sinking, but her recount does not have a conclusion. There is a real difference in tone between the two paragraphs: in the first she has worked at creating a sense of atmosphere and drama ('monstrous boat', 'deadly iceberg', 'very early in the morning'), while the second paragraph is a simple list of statistics without any attempt to bring them to life. She has included some of the information she knows, but her account is very limited, perhaps because of time constraints, although there is no sense that she has produced a detailed but unfinished account – rather, she seems to have selected information in a random way, without any planning of her recount. Her difficulty may be, as with Lucas, that she has no clear sense of the audience and purpose for her writing. She knows that her teacher, who will mark the work, and her classmates, who may also read it, all know as much as she does about the *Titanic*.

### Next steps for Emma

Emma, like Lucas, would benefit from a clear sense of an audience that knows nothing about the topic. This could be a real audience, such as younger children in the school, or an imagined audience, such as readers of newspapers at the time of the event. She needs to plan her writing so that she covers the events she is writing about systematically; in the case of chronological writing, this could be in the format of a timeline. Emma also needs to consider what to include in her introduction – the who, when, where, what formula could be helpful for her as well – and how to conclude her writing. It might appear that her recount has the same weaknesses as Lucas's, and that therefore they are at the same stage, but it is important to remember the added challenge of a recount of events one has not experienced.

# Instructions

The main features of instructions are:

- a structure consisting of the goal; a list of materials and equipment needed, if necessary; steps needed to achieve the goal, in sequence;

- steps numbered or bullet pointed to make them easier to follow;

- diagrams or illustrations if useful;

- imperative verb forms;

- adjectives and adverbs used to make instructions clearer.

Children are often encouraged to use adverbs of time such as 'first', 'next', 'finally' in instructions, but these are far less helpful for users in keeping track of where they are in the instructions than numbers.

## CHILDREN'S WRITING

Julia, year 2: How to make a Lego minion

**Equipment**

- bricks
- small red pieces

- eye piece
- glass piece
- shoulder pieces

**Method**

Step 1  First you get a yellow four piece with a stick on it.

Step 2  After you did that get a eye piece and put it on the stick.

Step 3  then get 4 thin shoulder pieces and put them under the head.

Step 4  Once that's done get a get a navy brick and lots of blue ones.

Step 5  next put the blue bricks in rows and the navy in the middle.

Step 6  then get two navy for the legs and put yellow for the arms under the sholder caps.

Step 7  finally display your Lego minion.

## COMMENTARY

Julia understands the structure of instructions and uses appropriate vocabulary for the headings of the different parts. Her instructions are quite concise but include necessary details such as the colour of the bricks. She uses the imperative mood consistently, but has a little difficulty with tense in the subordinate clause in step 2; in step 4 she manages it successfully. Her final step suggests a celebration of achievement, which works well.

## Next steps for Julia

Julia might consider how to improve her instructions by making them even more concise. She could remove any words or phrases that are not essential. Children often think that quantity of writing is a measure of quality; it is good for them to see that sometimes the opposite is true.

## CHILDREN'S WRITING

Marius, year 5: Rob the bank

The Game is Rob the banb. Get in the fun with Rob the bank go to jail or suvive.

*(Continued)*

(Continued)

Equipment

- Dice (tow)
- 5 yellow c
- ounters
- 5 blue counters
- 2 counters (any colour)

1. Initily you roll the dice and move the amount.
2. carry one until you reach the
3. if you land on go to jail instantly go
4. if you land on colecte coins, colect coins
5. if you land on the mumy go anwere between 15!
6. if you land on roll again roll agan

Who-ever wins has to wait whilst your oponant moves. Before that you'll have to Wait!

Marius was asked to improve starters of instructions: his first attempt follows.

2. Carry on until you reach the finish
3. when you land on jail instantly go
4. when you land on colect coins, colect coins
5. while your on the mumy go enihere between 15!
6. last when you land on roll again, roll again

He then made a second attempt.

1. initily, you roll the dice and move that amount.
2. Quitly, carry on until you reach the finish.
3. Whenever you land on go to jail instantly go.
4. Whilest your on a mumy, you can go anywer between 15.
5. So if you land on colect coins, colect coins

lastly, when you land on roll again, roll again.

## COMMENTARY

Marius, as with Julia, uses the structure of instructions and also language features such as the imperative form. The game appears to be a race game, and so the instructions do not really have to be in a specific order apart from the first two, as the others simply refer to different options for different squares on the race track. Indeed, it could be that some of the instructions are unnecessary as players presumably will see them on the squares as they land on them.

### Next steps for Marius

Marius was asked to redraft the starts of his instructions to avoid the repetition of the sentence opener in instructions 3 to 6. By year 5, children may be already recognising such issues if they read their work through, and perhaps even read it aloud to themselves or a writing partner. This critical rereading is very important in encouraging purposeful independent redrafting. In terms of whether the instructions work, asking other pupils to test them out is the best way to check whether anything is missing or any of what is included could be removed. Marius needs to be constantly aware of the needs of his audience and the purpose of his writing.

# Information writing (non-chronological reports)

The main features of non-chronological reports, which provide information about a topic, are:

* an introduction to the topic;

* information about the topic, selected for its relevance and interest, organised into different sections;

* a conclusion;

* often in the present tense and third person;

* precise descriptive language;

* possibly questions and comments to draw the reader in.

## CHILDREN'S WRITING

Leila, year 1: Non-chronological report

**Caterpillars**

*What do caterpills look like?*

*Most caterpillars have 3 pairs of true legs and 5 pairs of prolegs. They can be different sors.*

*What do catpillars eat and drinck?*

**Ladybirds**

*What do ladybirds look like?*

*They are red, black or yello. And there bright colours to scar away their enamies!*

*They are diffrent colours Spots dpending what sort of ladybirds it is.*

*What do ladybird eat?*

*They eat 500 greenflys a year and they are called gardnass frind.*

## COMMENTARY

Leila's report is divided into two main sections, each organised by the use of two questions as headings. This structure was provided for her, and it would have been interesting to see how she might have organised the information herself. She has not provided any information in response to the question 'What do caterpillars eat and drink?', perhaps because she could not remember the answer or because she ran out of time. Leila has selected the information that interests her most; her description of the animals' appearance focuses on one key aspect – caterpillars' legs and the colour of ladybirds. She includes additional facts that add interest to her report: that ladybirds' colours have a protective function and that they are known as gardeners' friends. She writes consistently in the present tense.

## *Next steps for Leila*

Leila could begin to organise her own non-fiction writing by devising her own questions to answer. This would allow her to focus on aspects of the topic which she finds most interesting, as well as introducing her to the planning process.

The following samples, from children three years older than Leila, show how they are able to produce much longer and more sophisticated pieces, and also how writing may not conform to the narrow view of text types. The samples consist essentially of a chronologically ordered sequence of mini-reports. The children have chosen which periods to include in their work.

| Connor, year 4 | Tiffany, year 4 |
|---|---|
| *Homes through the ages*<br>Homes are one of the most important things that you need in your life to survive. Homes keep you warm and protect you. | *Homes through the ages*<br>Homes have changed a lot throughout history, starting with Stone Age. Homes have been needed for a long time, people need homes for shelter, wormth and sleep. |
| *Stone age homes*<br>Stone age homes are built out of wattle and daub. Intrestingly, wattle and daub is dung and clay mixed together. They had thatched roofs. | *Stone Age*<br>At the start of stone age people were living in caves to keep away unwanted animals. They would usully build a fire in the middle of the cave for light and warmth. Later on in the stone age people were living in teepees made out of wooden posts tied together at the top with strong viens. They would rap animal skins around to make walls and roofs. |
| *Tudor homes*<br>Tudor people live in black and white homes. Traditionally., they had jettys and distinctive black and white. Oftenly, they have stone at the bottom then wattle and daub coated in limewash. | *Anglo Saxons*<br>Anglo Saxon homes were built in small villages with the hall in the middle of other peoples houses. The hall is where the chief lives and is the biggest. The houses were made out of wood planks for the walls and a thatched roof. They were one room with a fire in the middle, wich was very dangerous. Oddly, the anglo Saxons brought their animals inside when it was cold! They placed their villages near water and trees for building new houses and for the aimals. |

| Connor, year 4 | Tiffany, year 4 |
|---|---|
| *Modern homes*<br>Modern day homes are built of brick and cement. They use cement to stick the bricks together. They use big glass panels they also had a chimly. Intrestingly, very modern homes usally have 8 rooms. | *Tudor*<br>Interestingly, tudor homes had jettys witch overhung the level bellow! Tudor homes were made out of wattle and daub. Wattle is weaved sticks and daub is a mixture of manure, mud, clay and sand that hardens when it drys. Tudors used limewash to make the walls white and the Victorians used tar to make the beams black and to keep them from rotting. Tudor houses have small window panes, steep roofs, bay windows and thatched or tiled roofs. |
| I think homes have changed exeptionly imagine what it would be like in 100 years. | In the great fire of London many Tudor houses were burnt down because they were flamable. I wonder what future houses will be like. |

## COMMENTARY

It is noticeable that Tiffany has written more than Connor. This means that she is able to include far more information, which is important in a report. Both writers have included an introduction which makes general points about the topic and leads well into the main body of the writing. Tiffany's sections are much fuller and more wide-ranging, while Connor only writes about building materials. Both writers have brief conclusions which point to the future; Connor also draws a general conclusion, but Tiffany's reference to Tudor houses is not linked clearly enough to the final sentence. (Tiffany's vocabulary choices are discussed in Chapter 7.)

### Next steps for Tiffany and Connor

These pupils have managed the relatively simple structure of this topic well; essentially, the sections are chronologically ordered. They might now write about topics that cannot be structured in this way – for example, a topic such as Life in the Stone Age would be very open in terms of what information they might choose to include and therefore what sections they might use to organise that information (Stone Age homes, farming, family life, cave paintings, stone circles) and how they sequenced them.

# Explanations

The main features of explanations are:

- a general introduction to the subject being explained;

- a series of steps explaining how or why something happens (or a list of reasons that may not be in stepped sequence – for example, in an explanation of why the Vikings came to Britain);

- a conclusion;

- often written in the present tense, with causal conjunctions such as 'because', 'so', 'although';

- questions, exclamations or additional interesting information to draw the reader in.

## CHILDREN'S WRITING

Rhys, year 4: How the water cycle works

Do you know 70% of water is in the oceon. 90% of water is your brain Incredibul isn't it. And this is the water cycle works.

In the begining water is at the sea, and the sun comes out the trees rotts suck up the trunck and to the leves and up to the leaves and up into the air ...

Next the water vapour is in the sky and it forms a cloud, this is called condensation while its up in the air it goyns to more cloudes

The clouds can't hold much longer so it rains and falls on montins and ether goes under ground or over ground it is called run-off or ground waterflow.

Last of all the water goes back to the sea. The water cycle goes on and on and never stops. 70% of water is in your body. To find out more information go to: 'facts of the water cycle' from profeser of the Word of wonders.

## COMMENTARY

Rhys has used two surprising facts to hook his readers in, in question format and both followed by another question to suggest the reader's response. He then moves into the steps of the explanation, although he has some difficulty in linking these effectively at the beginning. His conclusion is appropriate (the water cycle goes on and on and never stops), but he does not seem to realise he is repeating the fact about the body, which in any case is not really appropriate here. The direction to further sources of information is typical of information texts. Rhys's explanation is concise and he explains subject-specific terminology such as 'condensation', 'run-off' and 'ground water flow'. (Rhys's punctuation is discussed in Chapter 8.)

### *Next steps for Rhys*

Rhys needs to ensure that every fact included in his writing is relevant to the topic and that he sequences all steps in explanations accurately. He might benefit from accompanying or even replacing his written account with a labelled diagram or flowchart; it is important that children learn to consider the most appropriate format for conveying information.

The next example of an explanation comes from a child a year older than Rhys.

## CHILDREN'S WRITING

Malia, year 5: From reservoir to tap

Have you ever wondered how your house gets water? Find out how water gets from reservoir to your tap by reading this explanation.

First, water from three different reservoirs called: Fewton, Swinsty and Thruscross makes its way to Eccup reservoir. Some water also comes from Moor Munkton where water from the Ouse is sived through a screen with 3mm gaps, to make sure that any wildlife dosen't come with the water. Then the water gets sived again, and gets colleted in Eccup reservoir. This process is called screening. Eventually, the water won't have any wildlife or debree in it and it can go on to the next stage.

Next, the water gets transported to the flash mixers where the water, and the bad things (baddies) get mixed together. Allum and sulphur dioxide gets added to the water to attract the baddies. There are 3 flash mixers that spin very fast to mix the water. Then, the water heads into the flocculator where flocc starts to form. Flocc is made of Peat, Algi, Bacteria, Cyclops, Water flea, Daphnia, and Protasoa.

After that, the water reaches the dissolved air flotation tank; using dissolved air to make the Flocc float to the top, the tank then uses brushes on a chain, conneted to a cog, to brush the Flocc off into a drain, leading to the sewers. It get rid of 85% of the flocc.

Nextly, the water goes to the rapid gravity sand filter. At the bottom of the tank ther's a layer of compressed plastic, then 1 meter of sand, and finally 2 meters to contain the water. Gravity makes the water move down through the sand and the plastic, takeing away the remaining 15% of the flocc.

Next, the water goes to the ozone tank, where using ozone gas gets rid of Pestiside and Herbiside. Then the water goes to the granular activated carbon filter that gets rid of the ozone gas, and any leftover Herbiside or/and Pestiside.

Finally, the water heads to the contact tank. The contact tank holds it until it jurneys through pipes to your house. To make sure the water is completely clean when you get it, 1/50 of clorine in a simming is added to the water. Therefore, if it comes across anything it will still be clean.

Now you know how water gets from reservoir to your house. You can also spread your knowledge to everyone you know.

## COMMENTARY

This long and impressive explanation shows how first-hand experience and secure knowledge of the topic can enhance writing. A visit to a water-treatment works, where the process was explained by an enthusiastic expert, meant that the class was very well informed about the topic and also keen to explain it to others. They knew that this was information that very few people would have, making their writing purposeful. Malia refers to this in her conclusion, suggesting that the reader should now be able to pass the information on to others. Her introduction is also brief and to the point, and, like Rhys, she uses a question to hook her reader in. She explains the many steps of the process carefully and in detail. In this long piece, adverbials of time (first, then, next, after that, finally) are used effectively to signpost the different stages.

### Next steps for Malia

Malia might also benefit from producing her explanation as a flowchart, as would be likely to happen in adult-produced texts on this topic. The process of moving towards a diagrammatic representation, in which there is space for little written text, would help her to select the most important information and also consider what can and cannot be represented visually. Malia might also try writing explanations that do not have a chronological structure – for example, why a settlement is in a particular place or why groups of invaders came to Britain.

# Persuasive writing

Persuasive writing is characterised by:

*   an opening claim or position statement;

*   arguments, often supported by evidence and examples;

*   a return to the original statement in the conclusion;

*   usually in the present tense, with causal conjunctions such as 'because';

*   possibly rebuttal of any arguments that could be made against the writer's viewpoint;

*   a friendly, reasonable tone and attempts to imply that the writer's view is widely shared;

*   use of humour or an emotional appeal;

*   strong, positive language, and use of language effects such as alliteration and short sentences for impact.

## CHILDREN'S WRITING

Christian, year 4: Renewable energy – the future!

Dear reader,

Have you heard about renewable energy? Many technology improvements have led to further uses of solar, wind and hydro energy. Just think about your children, how will they survive if the lights go out?

Face it, one day coal and gas will run out and leave us in a crisis. Do you want to help this dreadful fact? Well, what you could do is use a source of renewable energy instead of using fossil fuels. Two popular types are solar and wind energy.

Also, there is a lot more energy being used, switch to keep the bills down. Everyone hates the bills!!

Fossil fuels may cause severe problems like global warming as well as polution. Burning coal creates severe greenhouse gases. Air pollution can also cause major health problems, especially for young children and more so babies. Renewable energy, of course, does not cause pollution. Our Earth needs to be looked after and cared for, as if you were caring for yourself.

Renewable energy is extremely cheap to run. Why not try installing solar panels? They may be expensive to install but your money can be earnt back, especially in Summer. Same situation with wind power. Electronic cars perform as well as petrol/diesel whichever you own. Again your money can be earnt back with a charge point powered by renewables.

We all know that the renewables are economical, and even more With it being cheap, pollution free and readily available, I personally think that there are no excuses not to be using, - either now, or in the next few years. Everybody that I know has the ability to move on. In a few years, the renewables may be the latest craze. Let's think about tommorrow today!

Yours sincerely,

C___ J___

## COMMENTARY

Christian has included a number of arguments for renewable energy sources in his writing: that fossil fuels will run out, that they cause climate change and pollution, that renewables are cheap. These are generally quite well organised, although he does return to the cost question in two paragraphs as well as the conclusion. Each argument is stated clearly, sometimes with additional information – for example, on the effects of atmospheric pollution. He uses strong language to persuade the reader – 'crisis', 'dreadful fact', 'severe problems'. But the piece is overwhelmingly positive; rather than simply trying to frighten his audience, Christian aims to convince them that a switch to renewables is easy and the obvious choice. We do not know if he knows any of the counterarguments sometimes used; it may be that he simply decided to ignore them.

Christian moves between first and second person in his writing, sometimes addressing the audience as 'you' ('your children', 'do you want?'), but sometimes identifying himself with the audience ('leave us in a crisis', 'our Earth', 'we all know') and at the end making his own personal position clear ('I personally think', 'everybody that I know'). His language implies that his own viewpoint is generally shared ('we all know', 'everybody that I know'). This technique is often used in persuasive writing. He uses modal verbs on occasion to suggest levels of doubt or possibility ('what you could do', 'may cause', 'can also cause', 'may be expensive'), showing that he recognises the importance of not over-stating his argument. Imperative verbs ('just think', 'face it') add a forceful note to his language. Christian uses longer sentences to develop his points and shorter sentences ('Everyone hates the bills!' 'Same situation with windpower.') for emphasis. The second example, of course, is not a grammatically complete sentence, but it adds a slightly informal touch that can help to make the reader feel closer to the author. Christian finishes with a ringing call to action ('Let's think about tomorrow today!'), which one could imagine as the slogan for a campaign for renewable energy, although on closer inspection its heroic tone is matched by a vagueness worthy of a politician.

### Next steps for Christian

Christian's writing might benefit from more attention to structure and a clearer signposting of his arguments. In planning his writing, he could list his main points and then decide what would be the most effective way of sequencing them – strongest argument first or last? Is there a logical sequence that would allow the argument to develop rather than simply being a list of points? Once the structure is clear, he would be able to make it apparent to his reader through the use of devices to aid cohesion, such as 'There are three reasons why … ', 'Firstly', 'Finally'. He might also consider features of layout that would help to emphasise key points, such as bullet pointing or the use of text boxes. Children often enjoy developing the visual impact of their writing, and it is important to learn how such techniques can be used effectively.

# Discussions

Discussions typically have the following features:

- an introduction stating the question or topic to be discussed;

- arguments for and against, with supporting evidence;

- a summary of the arguments and a conclusion about the debate;

- usually written in the present tense;

- language of logic and reason – 'although', 'however', 'on the other hand';

- language of moderation and caution – 'may', 'might', 'often', 'sometimes'.

## CHILDREN'S WRITING

Scarlett, year 6: Should all zoos be closed down?

Zoos should be closed down because they disrupt animals' life styles. The animals do not get enough exercise and do not find food for themselves. The enclosures they live in are too small and don't have enough equipment for them to play with. The animals get bored and restless; birds in small enclosures fly around in circles, while in the wild they can fly in straight lines. Zoos do not help endangered species because the problem is that their habitats are being destroyed. Zoo animals are sometimes lonely because they are used to living in big packs but in zoos there is not enough space for them to live in big groups.

People who think zoos are good say that you can see animals you could never see in the wild, but you can see them on TV programmes in the wild. Some people think that a visit to the zoo is a good day out, but it isn't right for everyone to look at the animals and spy on them. Zoo animals can look really unhappy in their cages, which can make people think that they should be set free.

I think that animals should not have to suffer what we do not have to suffer, being put on show and living in cages.

## COMMENTARY

Scarlett has included a number of arguments for closing zoos, a subject she feels strongly about, and recognises some opposing views while countering them with her own opinions. She provides explanations and examples to develop her points, drawing on what she has read and her own experience. She has not provided any introduction other than the question, instead launching straight into her arguments against zoos, and her conclusion does not fully summarise her discussion. Scarlett tends to list her points without linking them through cohesive devices, including words and phrases such as 'also, however', 'in conclusion'. She does use some moderating language ('some people', 'can look').

## Next steps for Scarlett

Scarlett has had very little experience of this type of writing in her primary school career. She would benefit from more speaking and listening activities, including group and whole-class discussions and formal debates, and perhaps an approach such as philosophy for children, first developed by Matthew Lipman (1980), which supports children in learning to think critically and collaboratively, developing their ability to reason. She also needs opportunities to read and analyse examples of discursive writing, so that she has a model for the structure and language needed.

# Conclusion

As children move through their education, non-fiction writing becomes more and more important, affecting learning across the curriculum. It depends on their reading skills, as most non-fiction writing tasks are based on researching a topic, and evaluating and selecting information. Although becoming familiar with a range of different non-fiction text types supports children's writing, they will eventually begin to notice common features rather than the often less important surface differences. For example, non-fiction writing usually needs an introduction and a conclusion, and a logical structure for the main body of the piece. But beyond this, non-fiction writing has to respond to three basic questions.

- Audience: who is this writing aimed at? (This will influence both content and style.)

- Purpose: what is this writing trying to achieve?

- Form: based on the answers to the first two questions, what is the best way to organise this writing?

Of course, even skilled writers usually like to see examples of a non-fiction writing task which they have not tackled before, but children should not feel they have to follow a model slavishly. They should be encouraged to develop the confidence to make their own decisions about their own writing.

# References

Arnold, H (1999) "I want to find out": What is Involved in Reading for Learning? In Bearne, E (ed.) *Use of Language Across the Primary Curriculum*. London: Routledge.

Bearne, E (2002) *Making Progress in Writing*. London: RoutledgeFalmer.

Bearne, E and Reedy, D (2018) *Teaching Primary English: Subject Knowledge and Classroom Practice*. Abingdon: Routledge.

Corbett, P and Strong, J (2011) *Talk for Writing Across the Curriculum*. Maidenhead: Open University Press.

Lewis, M and Wray, D (1998) *Writing Frames: Scaffolding Children's Non-fiction Writing in a Range of Genres*. Reading: Reading and Language Information Centre, University of Reading.

Lipman, M. (1980) *Philosophy in the Classroom*. Philadelphia, PA: Temple University Press.

National Literacy Strategy (1998) *The National Literacy Strategy Framework for Teaching*. London: Department for Education and Skills.

National Strategies (n.d.) Progression papers. Available at: http://webarchive.nationalarchives. gov.uk/20110205214828/http://nationalstrategies.standards.dcsf.gov.uk/search/primary/results/ nav:45784 (accessed 6 July 2018).

# 5
# POETRY

## IN THIS CHAPTER

This chapter explores the assessment of children's poetry. It discusses the challenges of teaching and assessing poetry. It considers the structures and sequences that can be found in poetry.

Poetry can be difficult to assess because there is probably more subjectivity in judgements about it than any other form of writing. What appeals to one reader may leave another cold. What intrigues one reader may baffle another. Poetry may be highly structured in terms of rhyme scheme, rhythm and verse structure, or may be free verse. Poetry does not have to follow the usual rules when it comes to sentence structure and punctuation, and it can, of course, be nonsense. Invented words are permissible in poetry where they would not be in other forms of writing. In poetry, there may be an element of playing with language, or playing with images and ideas in a creative way. The challenge of assessing creativity, discussed in Chapter 1, is significant here. The constraints of working within a particular poetic form may encourage children to be more creative, or may overwhelm the writer and lead to a loss of meaning and vividness. Vocabulary choice is extremely important in poetry writing, but this does not mean the choice of obscure words: the most familiar words can be extraordinarily powerful when used carefully. 'Common', after all, can mean ordinary, but also shared, as in common land, and familiar words such as 'home' or 'journey' can carry a weight of meaning that the reader has access to. Carter (1998) suggests that as a result of the difficulties in assessing poetry, writing assessment has focused strongly on prose, and that this has affected the place of poetry in the English curriculum. This is regrettable, and it is important to consider carefully how poetry can be assessed, in part simply to redress this situation, but more importantly to support children's poetry writing effectively.

While poetry may often appear to be unstructured, we do in fact recognise when a poem has some sort of logical sequence and an ending that sounds like an ending, rather than the poem simply stopping. The ending is probably more important than the beginning; it works in the same way as a final chord in a piece of music, producing a sense of completion. A series of ideas or images can build towards a climax and resolution – for example, they may become more exaggerated through the poem or move from playful to serious.

In assessing poetry, we need to consider not only what techniques, such as the use of alliteration or similes, have been used, but also how successfully they have been used. Similes can be so over-used that they cease to have any power: consider, for example, 'as white as snow' or 'as cold as ice'. A good simile or metaphor has two elements; the first is an element of surprise, as the reader encounters an unexpected comparison, where perhaps there is only one similarity between the two things being compared. The second is an element of recognition – how close the similarity is. The aim is a reader's response of 'What? Oh, yes!' This is a good opportunity for originality, since it calls for a comparison that is new (no one has ever compared these two things before) and of value (it makes us see the two things afresh). It is captured very effectively in DJ Enright's poem *Blue umbrellas* (1981), which begins with a child's description of a peacock, *The thing that makes a blue umbrella with its tail*. One can imagine the child watching with fascination as the bird opens and closes its tail, and being reminded of the much more mundane opening and closing of umbrellas.

The first poem to be considered comes from an older writer.

## CHILDREN'S WRITING

Aidan, year 6: Those Birds of Steel

Those Birds of Steel,

How amazing they feel,

Twisting and turning through the sky,

as nimble as a dragon fly.

Now the Hun loom over London,

filled with bombs, ready to plunder

The drone of the engines means trouble,

Whole cities turned to rubble.

Bombers roar across the sky,

so many innocent people die,

fighter planes, so sleek, so swift,

swerving and speeding through the mist …

Oh, how many people died in the war,

for some people today it is just a bore,

how many brave young men put their lives at risk,

we can now look and hear about it, on a disc.

## COMMENTARY

Aidan is tackling a serious subject in this poem, and he draws on his knowledge about the war within it. As the title suggests, he focuses on the fighter planes. The title is also that of a video game, and it is likely that Aidan is familiar with the game, but it is a powerful image. Aidan describes the movement of the planes very effectively through the use of well-chosen verbs ('twisting', 'turning', 'swerving', 'speeding'). The dragonfly simile further develops our picture of the darting movement of the planes. He also creates a vivid picture of the bombers that 'loom' and 'roar'. The last verse picks up the references in the middle two verses to the impact of the bombing ('Whole cities turned to rubble', 'so many innocent people die') to reflect on the dwindling importance of the war today. This verse is arguably less successful than the rest of the poem; it is difficult to make the point that today we are somewhat distanced from the events of the war in as dramatic a way as he describes those events. The immediacy of the present tense in the first three verses is also lost as he moves to the present day and uses the past tense to refer to the war.

Aidan uses alliteration and rhyme effectively in his poem. He includes some near-rhymes – 'London' and 'plunder', 'swift' and 'mist' – and it is good that he does not feel constrained to seek out full rhymes throughout the poem. The only weaker note that seems to be driven by the search for rhyme comes at the very beginning, with the line 'How amazing they feel', where it is not clear whose viewpoint is being adopted, and at the end, where it is possible that the risk/disc rhyme drove the writing of the last two lines. The choice of the word 'plunder' might also have been affected by the desire to rhyme, since it is not really appropriate here, but it could also be that Aidan is not clear about its precise meaning. The alliteration ('loom over London; so sleek, so swift,/swerving and speeding') works well.

## *Next steps for Aidan*

Aidan is confidently manipulating key elements of poetry in his writing. He would benefit from opportunities to discuss his own and others' writing critically, to consider minor changes that would improve it and to evaluate its impact on the reader.

Younger writers are only beginning to develop the skills and confidence Aidan shows, as the next example (see p. 66) demonstrates.

## COMMENTARY

In the next poem, which William chose to write without any teaching input, he appears to be focusing on rhyme, with the content of the poem very much directed by his wish to end lines with a rhyme. His ideas almost appear more to be typical of information writing, consisting of a list of things he knows about fish. It is interesting, therefore, that he uses some near-rhymes rather than manipulating the writing until he has full rhymes throughout – so 'colours' and 'others' are rhymed, and also 'reeds' rhymed with 'seas' and 'peas', and 'bites' with 'light' and 'bright'. He does use an internal rhyme once – 'brains' and 'veins'. The drive to rhyme results in the unsuccessful simile in the first stanza (jelly fish compared to peas), but the lists in the same stanza work rather better, providing some pattern to the language.

---

### CHILDREN'S WRITING

William, year 2: Fish

Fish are many sorts of coulours,

Brown, Pink, gold and others,

You can find them in oceans, rivers, lakes and seas,

Jelly fish no brains, no vains no bones just like peas.

Sometimes you can't see much of the rivers because there's reeds

Gold fish are very bright,

But somtimes they are very light.

The bigest type of fish is a shark that bites.

---

## Next steps for William

William might benefit from activities with a strong focus on rhyme, to develop this skill while also thinking about meaning and rhythm. It might seem more sensible at this point to move away from rhyme, since it is constraining his writing quite significantly, but if children are interested in rhyme, it can be better to support them in using it effectively rather than discourage them from trying. For example, the model 'I'd rather be silver than gold' can be used as the basis of a poem, with words rhyming with gold generated and then the lines completed (e.g. 'I'd rather be young than be old, I'd rather be hot than be cold'). Once rhymes for gold have been exhausted, a different starter can be used (e.g. 'I'd rather be a door than a wall').

William might also enjoy using a rhyme-finder, which allows the writer to find all the single-syllable word rhymes for any given word.

## RHYME FINDER

| b | s |
|---|---|
| bl | sc |
| br | sl |
| c | sm |
| cl | sn |
| cr | sp |
| d | st |
| dr | sw |

| | |
|---|---|
| f | scr |
| fl | spr |
| fr | str |
| g | t |
| gl | tr |
| gr | v |
| h | w |
| j | y |
| l | z |
| m | ch |
| n | sh |
| p | shr |
| pl | th |
| pr | thr |
| r | |

It is important, of course, that children do understand that poetry does not have to rhyme, and that other language patterns can be used. This is evident in the next sample.

## CHILDREN'S WRITING

Carrie, year 4: How things change

I used to
climb in
but now I dive in

I used to
not know anything about Aztecs
but now I do

I used to be
7
but now I am 8

*(Continued)*

(Continued)

I used to
have 1 cousin
but now I have 2

I used to
not have any animals
but now I do

## COMMENTARY

Carrie has been given a simple and effective structure to work with, consisting of three-line verses in which the first and third lines start in the same way. This frame has freed her to consider significant changes in her and her life (Bearne and Reedy, 2018). The first two verses do this effectively by choosing a specific example to demonstrate an important change – her learning at school, and her growing confidence as shown by how she enters the swimming pool. This was unlikely to be intended as a metaphor but it could be read as one, and that would be useful feedback for Carrie. The last three verses are less successful, since they do not have implications relating to growing up (unless possibly she is only now trusted to look after pets). The rhyming of the last lines of the last two verses does, however, give a sense of completion to the end of the poem. It could be that Carrie used her best idea first, but it may also be that she did not have a clear enough understanding of what ideas would work well in this poem. She might also have thought about how she sequenced her ideas: the third verse might have been best placed at the beginning, with the first, and most powerful, saved for the end.

### Next steps for Carrie

As with Aidan, Carrie might benefit from shared and guided poetry writing sessions in which she can consider and evaluate her own and others' ideas, and be given feedback by other children and staff. She needs to be encouraged to reflect on the impact her writing might have on others.

The ability to reflect critically on writing and redraft it is significant in the writing process, and the next sample shows this clearly.

## CHILDREN'S WRITING

Rhiannon, year 2: By the fire - first draft
By the fire,
It ceeps me warm.

I watch the flames leap higher,

I stroke the cat,

On the mat.

By the fire – second draft

I sit by the fire,

And watch the flames leap higher.

I stroke the cat,

Asleep on the mat.

## COMMENTARY

This short poem was redrafted without any feedback from others, because the child herself was not satisfied with her first draft. It is worthwhile carefully considering the changes she decided to make. She has removed her second line entirely and reworked the first line, which did not fit well with what followed. The third line was then altered to follow on smoothly, since the new first line now has a subject and verb. The last line, which was too short, has been extended so that its rhythm matches that of the third line better. The poem now consists of two rhyming couplets, each with a slightly longer second line. Both couplets now start with 'I'. The language is therefore more success-fully patterned than in the first draft, and as a result the poem reads better. The subject of the poem is a fairly conventional one, perhaps one that the writer feels is appropriate to poetry.

### Next steps for Rhiannon

Rhiannon is clearly motivated to manipulate language in order to improve her writing. It might be helpful for her to try writing about her own experiences, in order to bring originality and freshness to her poetry.

## Poems based on models

Providing a model for children's poetry can be a useful way of supporting writing, but the choice of model is crucial. In the following example, the class had read WH Auden's *Night Mail*.

## COMMENTARY

Probably the most memorable feature of the original poem is the rhythm, which matches the relent-less drumming rhythm of the train's wheels on the tracks. Rhythm is often a neglected aspect of

## CHILDREN'S WRITING

Cora, year 5: The Midnight Train

the midnight train comes in to sight

Goes through the tunnel all eyes gleaming

they all want a letter but the

Midnight train goes on and on

but it must stop somewhere but

it does not stop one girl crying two

Boyes wondering if they could drive it

but the midnight train goes from

dusk till dawn and then stops at a

misty place and this is the End

of the midnight train

The

End

poetry writing, and children need careful support if they are to incorporate it successfully. In this example, Cora begins well, with a strong if not entirely regular rhythm in the first two lines, but then this breaks down. The rather odd line breaks between 'the' and 'midnight', 'but' and 'it', 'two' and 'boys', and so on may be a result of Cora focusing on the appearance of the poem rather than the sound, as in the handwritten original all the lines but the last are the same length.

## Next steps for Cora

Cora would benefit from reading aloud poems with strong rhythms, emphasising and even exaggerating the rhythmic beat. To support her writing she could work with models such as the one referred to earlier, 'I'd rather be silver than gold'. Each line must rhyme with the first, but in addition must maintain its rhythm. Beating out the rhythm of each line as it is composed helps writers to see where they might need to shorten or lengthen the line to maintain the rhythm – for example, 'I'd rather be bought than sold' needs to have an additional syllable, while 'I'd rather be timid than be bold' needs to lose the second 'be'.

Cora might then try writing poems with a strong rhythm but without rhyme, which is what she was attempting in 'The Midnight Train'. This would allow her to think about meaning and imagery as well as rhythm. It is important that writing activities provide an appropriate level of challenge. The model used is the key: a carefully selected model provides a balance of challenge and support, as can be seen in the next example, where the class had read a poem about a haunted house, in which each stanza focused on a different room in the house, listing objects in the room, and ending with a repeated line. Pablo has used this model to structure his own poem, and the class also looked at a set of photographs of rooms in old houses, and discussed them.

## CHILDREN'S WRITING

Pablo, year 2: The haunted house

In the cellar is …

A broken mangle

A stove with the fire blown out

A rabit hung from the ceeling

A washing tub

Some empty barrels

And the only sound is a strange wailing humming note.

In the nursery is …

A ripped picture of a baby

Some broken rattles on the floor

A bent Noah's Ark

And the only sound is a wailing humming note.

In the libary is …

A broken and blown out chandelier

A tattered Bibble whith pages torn out

A worn out mysterius skull of a mysterios Earl

And the only sound is a wailing humming note.

## COMMENTARY

It is worth noting that almost none of the objects Pablo describes were in the photographs he had seen, and indeed there was no photograph of a nursery, although there was some discussion of this option. In his original version, the cellar verse was the last and the library verse first; Pablo recognised that the poem worked better if he started with the more workaday objects in the cellar and built up to the skull. He conveys effectively the atmosphere of a possibly long-abandoned house, with hints of secrets and tragedies – the photograph ripped rather than accidentally torn, the damaged Bible, and the strange sound of unknown origin.

## Next steps for Pablo

As with previous examples, Pablo could be encouraged to discuss the effect his images and language create. He wrote the poem very fast and made no changes as he worked, and while this is not a problem in itself, it may mean that the reflection, which for some writers is part of the process of composition, is not something he does naturally. He might, for example, consider where he has used repetition intentionally and where it has happened by accident, and whether the poem might be improved by removing some of the repetitions. Sharing his work with others would give him a genuine audience response that would support his self-assessment.

Poetry writing may involve playing with rhythm, rhyme and other techniques, but it can also involve playing with ideas. The following poetry writing activity was inspired by a Valentine's Day group discussion recorded by Mary Jane Drummond, headteacher of a Sheffield infant school at the time (Drummond, 2012), in which the children considered who, or what, might send a Valentine to whom.

---

## CHILDREN'S WRITING

Karl, year 3: Valentine's Day poem

"I love you," said the twig to the bird,

"I love you," said the page to the word.

"I love you," said the wizard to the spell,

"I love you," said the witch to the smell.

"I love you," said the treasure to the chest,

"I love you," said the bird to the nest.

"I love you," said the bowl to the oat.

"I love you," said the paddle to the boat.

"I love you," said the d to the b,

"I love you," said the waves to the sea.

"I love you," said the front to the back,

"I love you," said the mouth to the snack.

"I love you," said the child to the sweet,

"I love you," said the drum to the beat.

---

"I love you," said the biscuits to the tin,

"I love you," said the rubbish to the bin.

"I love you," said the bulls eye to the dart,

"I love you," said the brain to the heart.

## COMMENTARY

The children wrote each line of their poem on a separate slip of paper, so they could then decide which way round to place the two lines in each couplet, and how to order the couplets, particularly which to put at the beginning and end of the poem. The simple structure allowed them to focus on the ideas, although the second line in each pair was constrained by the need to find a rhyme. Sometimes Karl aimed to find a second line linked in meaning to the first, as with the wizard/witch couplet, although this made for a less successful second line. In other pairings dictated only by the rhyme, the contrast between the ideas is striking – for example, the b/d line harked back to a discussion of letter reversals, a minor writing difficulty a world away from the image of endlessly rolling waves on the sea. The final couplet also works very well, with a suggestion that his images are hitting the target, and the brain which he uses to write the poem is paired with the heart which is its theme.

### Next steps for Karl

Karl enjoys playing with language and the challenge of a different type of writing. He is less ready to reflect on his writing and improve it, and would benefit from discussion of what works well and why. In this poem, it is interesting to think about the pictures the reader sees in the mind as they read, or the possible alternative meanings. For example, in the line about the drum and the beat, beat suggests violence and punishment – and yet the purpose of a drum is to give music its beat.

## Conclusion

Assessing poetry must go beyond a simple checklist approach – have similes and metaphors been used? have adjectives been used? does the poem rhyme? – if children are to learn what makes poems effective. As with baking a cake, it is possible to put in all the listed ingredients, but still not end up with a successful outcome. This is not to say that children should not learn about such features, noting them in poems they read and discussing how well they work, but being asked to include them when they do not naturally come into the writer's mind can be a recipe for stilted writing.

Auden (1948, p.170) wrote that *a poet is, before anything else, a person who is passionately in love with language*. That love of language, which is likely to lead to successful poetry writing, needs to be protected in those children who already have it and developed in those who do not.

# References

Auden, WH (1936) *Night Mail*. Available at: www.bbc.co.uk/learning/schoolradio/subjects/english/poetry/classic_poetry_2/night_mail (accessed 9 April 2018).

Auden, WH (1948) Squares and Oblongs. In Auden, WH, Shapiro, K, Arnheim, R and Stauffer, DA (eds) *Poets at Work: Essays Based on the Modern Poetry Collection at the Lockwood Memorial Library, University of Buffalo*. New York: Harcourt Brace & Co.

Bearne, E and Reedy, D (2018) *Teaching Primary English: Subject Knowledge and Classroom Practice*. Abingdon: Routledge.

Carter, D (1998) *Teaching Poetry in the Primary School: Perspectives for a New Generation*. London: David Fulton.

Drummond, MJ (2012) *Assessing Children's Learning*. London: Routledge.

Enright, DJ (1981) *Collected Poems*. Oxford: Oxford University Press.

# 6

# SENTENCE LEVEL ASPECTS OF WRITING: SENTENCE VARIATION

## IN THIS CHAPTER

This chapter explores grammatical aspects of writing, including sentence structure and how longer sections of text are linked. For each sample analysed there will be suggestions of next steps for the writer.

Sentences are the building blocks of written language. Over time, young writers learn to control and manipulate the sentence structure of the texts they produce. Particularly as they start to write longer texts, it is important to vary the structure of sentences to make the writing read better, and also for effect. For example, a short sentence in the middle of a series of longer sentences has a particular impact. A fronted adverbial, such as the following: 'At the stroke of midnight, she crept down the stairs' is more effective than 'She crept down the stairs at the stroke of midnight.' Conjunctions help to express a range of meanings: compare the following sentences.

Sam went home and no one was in.

Sam went home but no one was in.

Sam went home because no one was in.

Sam went home although no one was in.

The different conjunctions suggest very different possibilities: that Sam does or does not want company, that he is or is not surprised to find the house empty. The sentences could also be varied by using questions or exclamations.

Sam went home. Where had everyone gone?

Sam went home. How quiet the house was!

Typically, early writers write in short, simple sentences. However, some children continue to do this for much longer than others, and may need encouragement and support to write in longer sentences which make their writing read better and allow them to express more complex meanings. The following sample comes from a year 4 child; the writing will be analysed in terms not only of sentence length, but also sentence types – simple one-clause sentences, or sentences consisting of two or more clauses, with either coordinating or subordinating conjunctions joining the clauses. Finally, the sentence openings will be analysed, as variation here also makes writing read better, and the fronting of adverbials not only emphasises that element of the sentence, but also makes the text sound more like writing than like spoken language. Adverbials (words or phrases performing the function of an adverb, giving information about when, where or how the action of the sentence takes place) are highly mobile elements of sentences, which can often be placed at the beginning, middle or end.

This step-by-step full analysis of a piece of writing is unlikely to be needed very often, but it is intended to show that judgements about sentence structure are difficult to make unless the reader is able to identify clauses (which contain a verb) and, of course, it is also therefore necessary to be able to identify verbs and verb phrases accurately. This requires a good understanding of word classes: they are ways of categorising words according to their function within sentences, so often it is not possible to decide what class a word belongs to without reading it in a sentence. For example, many children would say confidently that the word 'kick' is a verb, and it fulfils that function in one of the two following examples, but not the other.

I kick the ball.

The last kick was the best one.

If children are taught that a verb is an action word, it is difficult for them to identify 'was' as the verb in the second sentence, where 'kick' is functioning as a noun. There is an added difficulty that sometimes a whole phrase fulfils the function of a verb.

I could have kicked the ball.

## COMMENTARY

First impressions of the following sample are probably that the writing does not read well; it has a jerky effect, and of course the lack of punctuation makes it more difficult to read. Analysis will show that the first impressions are correct.

## CHILDREN'S WRITING

Saffie, year 4: Harry Potter's diary

Dear diary,

I wish I did not live heer. I feall so annoyed and angry I wish I did not live here

I got shouted at by Auant I had not to burn the Bacon I felt so angry that I could blow up this house! now we've had breackfast now dudlys crying about his presents the phone rang it was about miss fig I was relifed then the door bell rang it was dudlys friend Dudly stopt crying (fake) then we lept into the car … and we went to the zoo and saw a gorilla it looked like duddly.

Then we went to the reptil House I saw a humungous boa constricta it winked at me then Dudly Pushed ME over then dudly fell in Vernon shouted HARRY! then I felt very proud that Dudly had fallen in the snake came slithoring out and around the floor

Then I got shouted at, we drove bace home Dudly felt embarresed. When we got Home …

Vernon locked me in my cupboard so now I am writing to you in my cupad I'am not allowed to have tea I am so bored in here.

The initial step in analysing the writing is to identify the sentences. They are often not demarcated by capital letters and full stops, but they are conceptual sentences that are grammatically complete, and that could therefore be demarcated without difficulty. The piece consists of 26 sentences, typically very short. The number of words is in brackets at the end of the sentence, and the verbs or verb phrases have been underlined (see the next example on p. 78).

## COMMENTARY

The average sentence length is eight words; there are two long sentences, of 20 words, three medium length sentences (11–13 words) and 20 consist of 7 or fewer words. Particularly where there is a series of short sentences, this leads to a rather jerky effect; longer sentences allow writing to flow better, while using short sentences (in moderation) for impact.

## CHILDREN'S WRITING

Dear diary,

I wish I did not live heer. (7)

I feall so annoyed and angry (6)

I wish I did not live here (7)

I got shouted at by Auant (6)

I had not to burn the Bacon (7)

I felt so angry that I could blow up this house! (11)

now we've had breackfast (5)

now dudlys crying about his presents (7)

the phone rang (3)

it was about miss fig (5)

I was relifed (3)

then the door bell rang (5)

it was dudlys friend (4)

Dudly stopt crying (fake) then we lept into the car … and we went to the zoo and saw a gorilla (20)

it looked like duddly. (4)

Then we went to the reptil House (7)

I saw a humungous boa constricta (6)

it winked at me then Dudly Pushed ME over then dudly fell in (13)

Vernon shouted HARRY! then I felt very proud that Dudly had fallen in (13)

the snake came slithoring out and around the floor (9)

Then I got shouted at, (5)

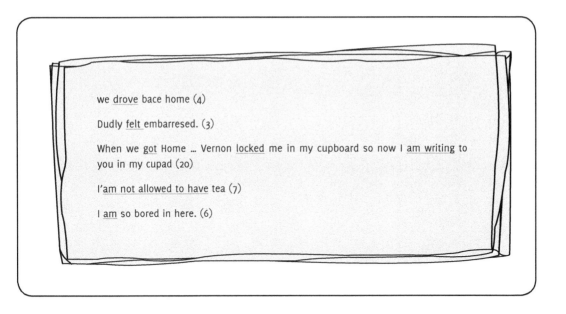

we <u>drove</u> bace home (4)

Dudly <u>felt</u> embarresed. (3)

When we <u>got</u> Home … Vernon <u>locked</u> me in my cupboard so now I <u>am writing</u> to you in my cupad (20)

I'<u>am not allowed to have</u> tea (7)

I <u>am</u> so bored in here. (6)

The next stage in analysing sentences is to check the number of verbs or verb phrases in each sentence. Where there is only one verb, the sentence is a single-clause sentence (often referred to as a simple sentence, though the National Curriculum programme of study (DfE, 2013) expresses a concern that this terminology can be confusing). Where there are two or more verbs, there are two or more clauses. The conjunction or conjunctions joining the clauses need to be identified. They are in bold in the next version of the writing.

## CHILDREN'S WRITING

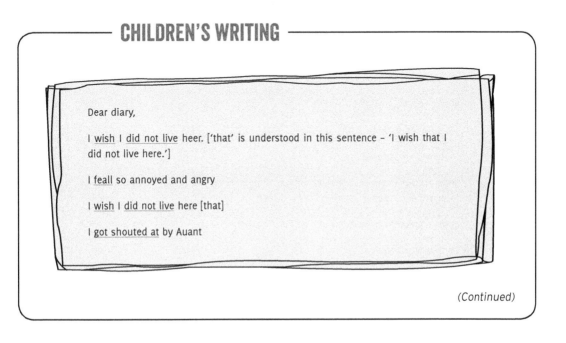

Dear diary,

I <u>wish</u> I <u>did not live</u> heer. ['that' is understood in this sentence – 'I wish that I did not live here.']

I <u>feall</u> so annoyed and angry

I <u>wish</u> I <u>did not live</u> here [that]

I <u>got shouted at</u> by Auant

*(Continued)*

(Continued)

I had not to burn the Bacon

I felt so angry **that** I could blow up this house!

now we've had breackfast

now dudlys crying about his presents

the phone rang

it was about miss fig

I was relifed

then the door bell rang

it was dudlys friend

Dudly stopt crying (fake) **then** we lept into the car … **and** we went to the zoo **and** saw a gorilla

it looked like duddly.

Then we went to the reptil House

I saw a humungous boa constricta

it winked at me **then** Dudly Pushed ME over **then** dudly fell in

Vernon shouted HARRY! **then** I felt very proud **that** Dudly had fallen in

the snake came slithoring out and around the floor

Then I got shouted at,

we drove bace home

Dudly felt embarresed.

**When** we got Home … Vernon locked me in my cupboard **so** now I am writing to you in my cupad

I'am not allowed to have tea

I am so bored in here.

## COMMENTARY

If the conjunction is a coordinating conjunction ('and', 'but', 'or', 'so', and much less often used, 'for', 'nor', 'yet'), the clauses are of equal weight in the sentence. Any other conjunction will be a subordinating conjunction and the subordinate clause, introduced by the conjunction, is dependent on the main clause. Sentences may contain both coordination and subordination – which is the case with two sentences here. There is some debate over whether 'then' can be used as a coordinating conjunction, but it does seem to fulfil that function in some of Saffie's longer sentences.

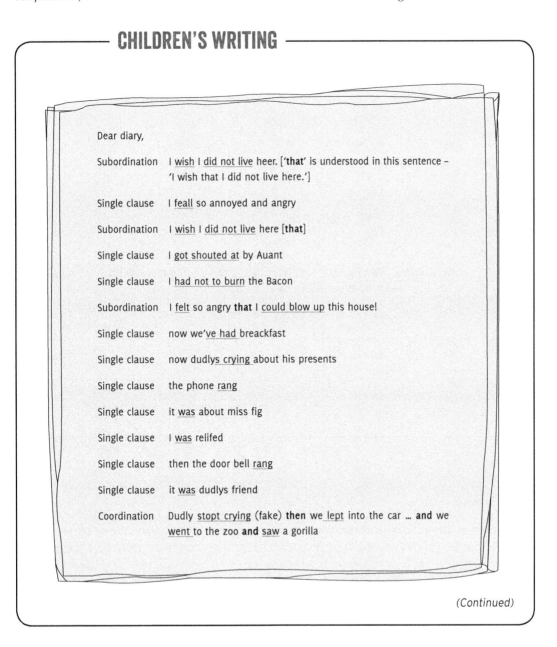

## CHILDREN'S WRITING

Dear diary,

| | |
|---|---|
| Subordination | I <u>wish</u> I <u>did not live</u> heer. ['**that**' is understood in this sentence – 'I wish that I did not live here.'] |
| Single clause | I <u>feall</u> so annoyed and angry |
| Subordination | I <u>wish</u> I <u>did not live</u> here [**that**] |
| Single clause | I <u>got shouted at</u> by Auant |
| Single clause | I <u>had not to burn</u> the Bacon |
| Subordination | I <u>felt</u> so angry **that** I <u>could blow up</u> this house! |
| Single clause | now we've <u>had</u> breackfast |
| Single clause | now dudlys <u>crying</u> about his presents |
| Single clause | the phone <u>rang</u> |
| Single clause | it <u>was</u> about miss fig |
| Single clause | I <u>was</u> relifed |
| Single clause | then the door bell <u>rang</u> |
| Single clause | it <u>was</u> dudlys friend |
| Coordination | Dudly <u>stopt crying</u> (fake) **then** we <u>lept</u> into the car … **and** we <u>went</u> to the zoo **and** <u>saw</u> a gorilla |

*(Continued)*

(Continued)

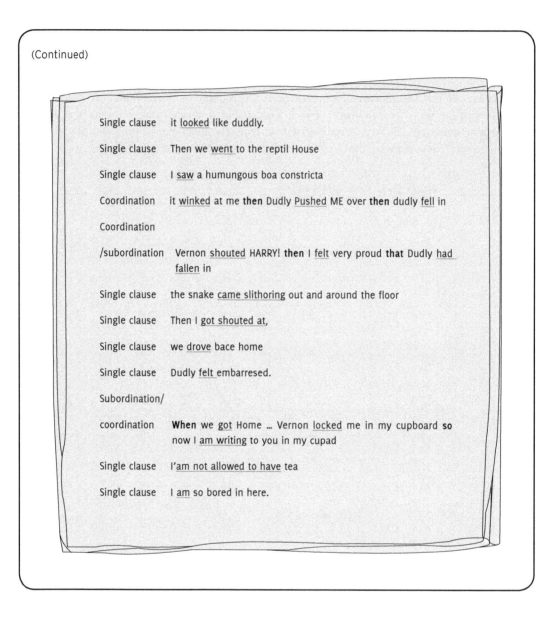

| | |
|---|---|
| Single clause | it <u>looked</u> like duddly. |
| Single clause | Then we <u>went</u> to the reptil House |
| Single clause | I <u>saw</u> a humungous boa constricta |
| Coordination | it <u>winked</u> at me **then** Dudly <u>Pushed</u> ME over **then** dudly <u>fell</u> in |
| Coordination | |
| /subordination | Vernon <u>shouted</u> HARRY! **then** I <u>felt</u> very proud **that** Dudly <u>had fallen</u> in |
| Single clause | the snake <u>came slithoring</u> out and around the floor |
| Single clause | Then I <u>got shouted at,</u> |
| Single clause | we <u>drove</u> bace home |
| Single clause | Dudly <u>felt</u> embarresed. |
| Subordination/ | |
| coordination | **When** we <u>got</u> Home ... Vernon <u>locked</u> me in my cupboard **so** now I <u>am writing</u> to you in my cupad |
| Single clause | I'<u>am not allowed to have</u> tea |
| Single clause | I <u>am</u> so bored in here. |

## COMMENTARY

This analysis matches the sentence length analysis; 19 of the sentences are single-clause sentences, two have coordinated clauses, three contain subordinate clauses and two contain both coordinated and subordinate clauses. It is important to note that very long sentences may be single-clause sentences, while multi-clause sentences can be relatively short. Look at the following examples.

'Late in the afternoon, on a bench outside the vast central bus station, <u>sat</u> a tiny hunched figure in a huge grey overcoat, ancient navy woollen hat and filthy pink gloves.' (a single-clause sentence)

'I <u>hid</u> **because** I <u>was</u> scared.' (main clause with subordinate clause)

Saffie uses a limited range of conjunctions: that, and, then, when.

The next aspect to analyse is the way in which the writer starts sentences. The vast majority start with the subject (20 sentences): of these, 14 start with a pronoun (ten with 'I', four with 'it') with the remainder starting with a proper noun (Dudley or Vernon) or a simple noun phrase ('the phone', 'the snake'). The other six sentences start with a fronted adverbial of time, but three of these are the single word 'then' (also used to connect clauses within two sentences) and two are 'now', with the other example being the subordinate clause 'When we got home'. Again, the repetition of sentence openers, particularly the repetition of 'I' in the first six sentences, adds to the jerky effect.

## Next steps for Saffie

Of course, Saffie needs to learn to demarcate her sentences with appropriate punctuation, which is considered in Chapter 8. However, from the point of view of sentence structure, the priority is to join more of her short sentences, using a range of conjunctions, and to use more varied sentence openers. This is best done in the context of Saffie's own writing; at the redrafting stage, she needs to read her work aloud and listen to the effect of the short sentences. She could then identify pairs of sentences that could be successfully linked and select appropriate conjunctions. Saffie should then reread the work to hear the difference. She could also look for sentences where a fronted adverbial would improve the writing – for example, 'The phone rang' or 'We drove back home'. Again, rereading aloud is important, to help Saffie hear the difference in the flow and rhythm of the writing. This approach would need to be used on a regular basis, and a thoughtful writing partner might be able to help with this.

While by year 4 children might be expected to have moved beyond writing in a series of short, simple sentences, it is important to remember that in the early stages this is very typical, and teachers should not rush children into attempting to join sentences too early, as they may not be able to hold longer, more complex sentences in their heads while transcribing them. However, as in spoken language, children often move on to a stage where a series of clauses is linked together with the coordinating conjunction 'and'. This can be seen in the following story by a year 1 child.

## CHILDREN'S WRITING

Cesilie, year 1: The blue whale

One day me and harreit went on a Boat and we were going to Scotland and harrieit fellover Bord and I cryed for help and a whale came and it was a freaidly whale and it culd fly and it went under wate and it Got harreit out and took her ashore she stayet there and till it took me and the Boat ashore and it took us home and harreit came home with me and we had some tea and went to Bed.

*(Continued)*

(Continued)

Although Cesilie has not demarcated the boundary, there is actually a sentence break in this story, but it does consist of two extremely long sentences. In the next version, the break has been put in and the conjunctions are underlined.

One day me and Harriet went on a boat <u>and</u> we were going to Scotland <u>and</u> Harriet fell over board <u>and</u> I cried for help <u>and</u> a whale came <u>and</u> it was a friendly whale <u>and</u> it could fly <u>and</u> it went under water <u>and</u> it got Harriet out <u>and</u> took her ashore. She stayed there <u>until</u> it took me and the boat ashore <u>and</u> it took us home <u>and</u> Harriet came home with me <u>and</u> we had some tea <u>and</u> went to bed.

## COMMENTARY

The first sentence is 53 words long and the second 31. 'And' is used 13 times to join clauses (note that it is also used twice to join words or phrases – 'me and Harriet', 'me and the boat') and the only other conjunction used is 'until' (which Cesilie thinks is 'and till').

## *Next steps for Cesilie*

Cesilie needs to recognise how she has structured her writing and this can be done by reading it aloud. There is no need to emphasise the 'and's or to attempt to read the work without taking a breath; readers should always attempt to read texts well, and it is possible to pause between clauses. However, even a serious attempt at reading the writing well will show up the repetition of 'and' as an issue. Cesilie might then be asked to highlight the word in order to reinforce how often it has been used and to start to consider how to improve the writing. The most straightforward strategy is simply to put in more sentence breaks. The next strategy is to try changing some of the conjunctions – for example, 'Harriet fell over board <u>so</u> I cried for help'. Some more radical restructuring could then be considered – for example, removing the repetition to produce 'and a friendly whale came', or 'and after we had had some tea we went to bed'.

Cesilie needs to understand that this redrafting is a normal – and important – part of the writing process and that all writers need to work at their writing in this way. She may need support with varying her sentence structures for some time, but it may well be that different writing tasks, which are not chronologically organised, would also encourage her to break up her sentences more and use a wider range of conjunctions.

Many children learn to vary sentences skilfully, whether consciously or not, producing well-structured writing that reads aloud well. This can be seen in an analysis of a year 6 pupil's diary entry, writing in role.

In the second version, the writing has been analysed as with previous samples: separated into sentences, with verb chains underlined and conjunctions in bold. Number of words in each sentence has been added.

## CHILDREN'S WRITING

Alfie, year 6: Word War II diary

Dear diary,

While I am writing now I am staring death in the face. Bombs are falling around me everywhere. If this goes on much longer I think I might go deaf. But my heart has already broken, my sister was killed by falling rubble on the way here. This night has gone so slowly I wonder if it will ever end. I can hear fires crackling all over above my head, and the peircing wail of the siren ringing in my ears. I can also hear people shouting and screaming, men and women. Anti aircraft guns are madly hurling their fill at the German bombers, but rarely hitting. When one does hit, though, you can hear the planes screeching as their flaming wreckage plummets through the sky hitting with the same effect as a small meteor. My mum is distraught, crying and rocking herself backwards and forwards. I kneel down and comfort her. My grandpa is a different matter, sitting on the platform and looking up into space, not saying a word. I just hope it will be over soon, this night and the war.

## CHILDREN'S WRITING

Dear diary,

**While** I <u>am writing</u> now I <u>am staring</u> death in the face. (12)

Bombs <u>are falling</u> around me everywhere. (6)

**If** this <u>goes on</u> much longer I <u>think</u> **[that]** I <u>might go</u> deaf. (12)

**But** my heart <u>has</u> already <u>broken</u>, my sister <u>was killed</u> by falling rubble on the way here. (17)

*(Continued)*

(Continued)

This night <u>has gone</u> so slowly **[that]** I <u>wonder</u>

**if** it <u>will</u> ever <u>end</u>. (13)

I <u>can hear</u> fires crackling all over above my head, and the peircing wail of the siren ringing in my ears. 21)

I <u>can</u> also <u>hear</u> people shouting and screaming, men and women. (11)

Anti aircraft guns <u>are</u> madly <u>hurling</u> their fill at the German bombers, **but** rarely <u>hitting</u>. (14)

**When** one <u>does hit</u>, though, you <u>can hear</u> the planes screeching **as** their flaming wreckage <u>plummets</u> through the sky hitting with the same effect as a small meteor. (28)

My mum <u>is</u> distraught, crying and rocking herself backwards and forwards. (11)

I <u>kneel</u> down **and** <u>comfort</u> her. (6)

My grandpa <u>is</u> a different matter, sitting on the platform and looking up into space, not saying a word. (19)

I just <u>hope</u> **[that]** it <u>will be</u> over soon, this night and the war. (13)

## COMMENTARY

Taking sentence length first, Alfie's average sentence length is 14 words, as compared with Saffie's 8. There are two short sentences of only 6 words, placed between longer sentences. The longest sentence is 28 words, and it could be argued that this sentence rather loses its initial impact, particularly with the description of the meteor as 'small'. Alfie uses a range of conjunctions, both coordinating (and, but) and subordinating (while, if, when, as). In three sentences the subordinate clause comes first. The majority of the sentences begin with the subject, 'I' in four sentences, and the others simple noun phrases.

A feature of Alfie's writing which should be noted is his frequent use of non-finite clauses, which add to the complexity and effectiveness of the writing. Non-finite verb forms are not limited by tense, person or number, as the following examples show.

I like <u>to dance</u>.

I went home, <u>skipping</u> all the way.

<u>Posted</u> on Monday, the first class letter arrived on Friday.

Alfie uses non-finite clauses in the following sentences, in which the non-finite verb has been underlined:

I can hear fires <u>crackling</u> all over above my head, and the peircing wail of the siren <u>ringing</u> in my ears.

When one does hit, though, you can hear the planes <u>screeching</u> as their flaming wreckage plummets through the sky <u>hitting</u> with the same effect as a small meteor.

My mum is distraught, <u>crying</u> and <u>rocking</u> herself backwards and forwards.

My grandpa is a different matter, <u>sitting</u> on the platform and <u>looking</u> up into space, not <u>saying</u> a word.

## Next steps for Alfie

With older and more skilled writers, it is important that they become independent in their ability to evaluate their own work, checking that the writing flows, that it reads well, that meaning is clear, and that the writing has the intended impact. Mature writers typically return to their writing to make these checks, often several times. They also recognise the importance of having others read their work to make the same checks but with fresh eyes. Alfie will benefit from regular opportunities to return to pieces of his writing with other children and with his teacher, and to redraft where necessary.

# Cohesion

Writing which reads well has variety in its sentences, and in particular variety in how sentences begin and how long they are. Questions and exclamations can also add to the quality of the writing. However, there are also some aspects of writing that are of the 'boring but necessary' kind, and these are elements of cohesion, which make the writing hold together well. These include consistency of tense and person (younger writers in particular sometimes switch between present and past tense, and first and third person narration), appropriate use of pronouns, and use of cohesive elements such as conjuncts. These are adverbials that link clauses, sentences and paragraphs, such as 'however', 'meanwhile', 'to conclude', 'nevertheless', 'therefore', 'on the other hand'. Lindley Murray, the eighteenth-century grammarian, described these as the hinges, tacks and pins of language, holding other elements together (Murray, 1797). These elements may be managed effectively in the first draft, but if not, reading the work through should show what changes need to be made to ensure cohesion. The example that follows shows issues of tense changes.

---

## CHILDREN'S WRITING

Morgan, year 6: Rainforest description

As I **turned** the corner I **see** a lovely stream with rocks covered in thick green moss

    past            present

beside it. I **walked** on, a huge bromeliad **stopped** me in my path. Hanging by the

         past                   past

bromeliad there **are** vines handing lifelessly on the branch. The air **was** humid, As I

        present                       past

**approach** the next corner I **see** cotton white fog. On one of the mossy rocks I **see** a

present          present               present

bright green slightly-camoflouge millipede slithering across the soft moss. On my

right I **see** tall towering trees with furry leaves surrounding the bare tree alone. giving

    present

it a warm coat.

## COMMENTARY

Morgan changes tense five times before settling into the present. He seems to take time to decide which will be the most effective form for this piece. Drafting allows for this work in progress approach. (This sample is also discussed in the next chapter, in terms of Morgan's vocabulary choices.)

### Next steps for Morgan

As with the previous samples, reading the work through, whether to himself or aloud with a partner, should help Morgan to identify the issue quickly, and to make a final decision about tense. It is important that children take responsibility for editing their own writing.

## Difficulties with sentence structure

When reading children's writing, it is relatively common to come across passages that are not written in grammatical sentences – perhaps because some elements have been left out or repeated, or because the structure is flawed. There is an important distinction between such writing and writing in which the punctuation is missing or misplaced. If the child is writing in grammatical sentences, it is quite straightforward to add punctuation; if they are not, it becomes difficult or impossible to punctuate the work without first changing it, as the next example shows.

## CHILDREN'S WRITING

Maisie, year 4: Science investigation: what blocks sound?

What I will do

I am Going to do ear muffs idea some one have the [radrir] on ear muff will be made cotton wool and see if can hear or not I'll get a same size bit of cotten I will get to bag of maddy and it my ear and see if can hear or not I am Going to a bit wood and put it on ear the same size a

## COMMENTARY

Maisie probably has a clear idea of how she plans to carry out her investigation, but she cannot explain it effectively in writing. This is probably because she appears to omit many words, particularly simple words such as pronouns and determiners; an example of this is:

**The** ear muff**s** will be made **of** cotton wool and **I will** see if **I** can hear or not

### *Next steps for Maisie*

Maisie would probably find it very difficult to repair her writing on her own, and would benefit from having support with reading it through and revising it so that it makes sense. She also needs to learn to reread constantly as she writes to check what she has written; it is much easier to do this than to leave all the checking to the end, when she may have forgotten what she was trying to say at the beginning. Teacher modelling of rereading during writing would be helpful; Maisie needs to understand that this is what skilled writers do.

Other examples of difficulties with sentence structure – writing that consists largely of short simple sentences, or short simple sentences chained together with 'and' or 'and then' can be seen earlier in this chapter. However, older or more experienced writers may also have difficulties with varying sentence structure appropriately. This can simply be an over-use of a feature such as the fronted adverbial. Any potentially effective technique can be ruined by constant repetition. Thriller writers who think that since short sentences can have impact, their writing will be improved by writing largely in very short sentences and paragraphs have missed the point. There is also an issue with sentences that become so long and complicated that both the writer and the reader get bogged down in them. For all these issues, rereading, preferably aloud, is the way to identify the problem, and after redrafting, reading again to check that the work now reads well.

# Conclusion

It is very common now for children to be given success criteria for their writing that focus on the inclusion of grammatical features such as subordinating conjunctions, fronted adverbials, or even the use of modal verbs or the passive tense. This may be a result of anxiety about children meeting the 'expected standard', as outlined in the assessment frameworks (Standards and Testing Agency, 2018a, b), where we find such indicators as the following.

- Year 2: use coordination (e.g. or/and/but) and some subordination (e.g. when/if/that/because) to join clauses.

- Year 6: use passive verbs to affect how information is presented; use modal verbs to suggest degrees of possibility.

But indicators are intended to be just that – indicators of writing skills and understanding – not ingredients for pieces of writing. There is a real danger that the strategy of requiring children to use particular grammatical structures inhibits them and produces awkward writing in which the writers are not able to focus properly on the big questions of 'What do I want to say?' and 'How can I say it effectively?' Children writing a story should be thinking about character, setting, plot and atmosphere, not how they can fit in a subordinate clause. Adult writers do not do think about grammatical structures and effects; they use them quite unconsciously. However, the successful writers who made public statements about their ignorance of fronted adverbials (Mansell, 2017) were perhaps missing the point. The issue is not whether children should be taught about grammar, but why and how. A review of research into grammar teaching (Andrews *et al.*, 2004) showed that formal grammar teaching appeared to have no impact on the quality of children's writing, but that teaching sentence combination, as suggested earlier for Saffie, was an effective way of developing children's use of more complex sentence structures. Traditional teaching which gives a definition, follows this with a few carefully prepared examples and exercises, and then asks children to incorporate the feature into their own writing, appears unlikely to succeed. This approach is perhaps sometimes a consequence of teachers not having confidence in their own subject knowledge, particularly since the increased demands in terms of grammar of the 2014 curriculum. However, an

## IN THE CLASSROOM

- If children read high-quality texts and investigate how they work, they begin to understand the techniques that successful writers use, and also to realise that it is useful to have labels for the features they find.
- If teachers then plan writing tasks in which a grammatical feature is likely to occur, such as subordinating conjunctions in an explanation, children are more likely to use them, particularly if teachers model this in shared writing.
- If pupils then have the opportunity to read through and reflect on their own writing, it is at this stage where the need to vary and refine sentence and text structure becomes obvious.

alternative approach is needed. Myhill *et al.* (2013) suggested that to be effective, grammar should be taught in the context of writing, using real examples, discussion and experimentation, and always with the focus on how to improve writing.

The National Curriculum programme of study is, in fact, quite explicit on this aspect of the writing process, stating, as was seen in Chapter 1, that pupils should reread their work to check for sense, revise it, edit it and evaluate it for effectiveness. We need to show children how to take as much pleasure and pride in the polishing stage of writing as in the planning and first draft stages.

# References

Andrews, R, Torgerson, C, Beverton, S, Freeman, A, Locke, T, Low, G, Robinson, A and Zhu, D (2004) *The Effect of Grammar Teaching (Sentence Combination) in English on 5–16 year olds' Accuracy and Quality in Written Composition*. Review summary. University of York.

Department for Education (DfE) (2013) *The 2014 Primary National Curriculum in England*. Eastleigh: Shurville Publishing.

Mansell, W (2017) Battle on the adverbials front: grammar advisers raise worries about Sats tests and teaching. *The Guardian*, 9 May. Available at: www.theguardian.com/education/2017/may/09/fronted-adverbials-sats-grammar-test-primary (accessed 9 July 2018).

Murray, L (1797) *English Exercises*. York: Wilson, Spence & Mawman.

Myhill, D, Jones, S, Watson, A and Lines, H (2013) Playful Explicitness with Grammar: A Pedagogy for Writing. *Literacy*, *47*(2): 103–11.

Standards and Testing Agency (2018a) *Teacher Assessment Frameworks at the End of Key Stage 1*. London: Department for Education.

Standards and Testing Agency (2018b) *Teacher Assessment Frameworks at the End of Key Stage 2*. London: Department for Education.

# 7

# VOCABULARY CHOICE

┌─────────── IN THIS CHAPTER ───────────┐

This chapter considers children's vocabulary choices in writing, and the impact these choices have on the quality of their writing.

└────────────────────────────────────────┘

Vocabulary choice can make a significant difference to the quality of writing. A well-chosen word can be as satisfying as a dart hitting the bull's eye, or can linger in the mind in the way a tune lingers in the ear. Less well-chosen words may either have no impact, producing colourless, pedestrian writing, or may actually jar on the reader – a word that is out of step with the rest of the writing in terms of style or mood can have a negative impact on the overall effect. Children who are getting to grips with the power of words may start by using only the simplest of vocabulary, then go to the opposite extreme by loading their writing with adjectives and adverbs, and using thesauruses without being familiar enough with the words they find to make good choices. Some words popular with children have the opposite impact to the one intended: *spooky*, for example, is too obvious to create any sense of mystery. No adult writer of ghost stories would dream of using it: they know they need to hint rather than spell out. Another issue is the 'one word good, two words better' approach. A child who writes 'the dark, black sun' has created a potentially striking (though puzzling) image, but either 'the dark sun' or 'the black sun' would work better; as it is, the two adjectives work against each other, too close in meaning to work together. We may be happy to accept 'The great big enormous turnip' as a title of a story for young children, but generally one carefully chosen adjective to suggest size is better than a series, especially when words such as 'ginormous' and 'humungous' are used.

In non-fiction, technical vocabulary creates an additional challenge for writers: children are encountering new words attached to topics and are expected to use them immediately and accurately. In a similar fashion, fiction writing with a historical setting requires children to use vocabulary appropriate to the period, and this involves knowledge about language that many primary age children simply do not have. It may be easier for them to avoid historical anomalies in the details of their stories, such as modern technology, than to avoid words and phrases that were not current even fifty years ago. Olinghouse and Wilson (2013) found that children in upper Key Stage 2 were able to choose vocabulary appropriate to the genre, and that this had an impact on the quality of their writing, so that information writing that made use of subject-specific vocabulary was likely to be good, while the quality of stories was linked to a wide and varied vocabulary.

There is huge variation in children's vocabulary, depending on what they are exposed to at home, and increasingly, as they grow older, how much and what they read. An American study (Hart and Risley, 1995) showed an enormous difference between the number of words a child growing up in a disadvantaged family heard in the first years of life compared with a child from an advantaged background. They called this the '30 million word gap by age 3' and demonstrated the impact not only on the size of children's vocabulary, but also the rate at which new words were learned, and language skills and reading comprehension at age 9 or 10. But the impact on writing can also be seen clearly; children with less extensive vocabularies simply have fewer tools at their disposal.

Assessing vocabulary choice involves not only considering the range of children's vocabulary, but also how well it is used. Sometimes very simple words are used extremely effectively; repetition of particular words can work very well and also very badly. We start by considering a sample fairly typical of a younger writer, in terms of vocabulary used.

## CHILDREN'S WRITING

Oliver, year 1: Story

Alfie and Annie Rose were in the puke [park] and they went on the swings and they went on the slaid and they went home. and At home they had a Suppa and for there pudding they had raise pudding for theer puhing. !!The end!!

## COMMENTARY

Oliver's word choices in this story are simple, with *went* and *had* used several times, and no use of adjectives and adverbs. He does not as yet have any sense of consciously choosing words to create an effect.

## *Next steps for Oliver*

It might seem that the next step to help Oliver improve his writing would be to encourage him to use adjectives. However, if one looks at where these could be placed, none of the nouns (park, swings, slide, supper, rice pudding) except perhaps rice pudding could be modified by adjectives in a way that would be manageable for a writer at this stage and would improve the quality of the writing. While the slide might be described as slippery, for example, that is only what one expects of a slide, and it is hard to think of any word to describe swings effectively in this context. The park could be big, but it is difficult to argue that this improves the story, other than ticking the adjectives box. The rice pudding could be described as delicious, but in a sense we infer that Alfie and Annie

Rose saw it as the highlight of the supper since it is the only item that is mentioned. Oliver could make his story more interesting by adding not single words but details, such as the weather and time of day (One sunny morning, one cold afternoon), or something that happened while the children played: perhaps they stayed on the swings until they felt dizzy; perhaps Alfie felt scared at the top of the big slide.

As children mature as writers, and as they read more extensively, and read more challenging texts, and their own vocabulary continues to develop, they have a much wider choice of words to draw on. The contrast between Oliver's story and the extract that follows from Theresa, three years older, is very marked, but Theresa's vocabulary choices are still not consistently appropriate or effective.

## CHILDREN'S WRITING

Theresa, year 4: extract from a story: Go home to Aus!

The tornado got closer and closer. Unexpectedly, the tornado rapidly swiped Rose's tree house off the ground. Rose was swirling and spining, gracefully swirling and spining. Suddenly she landed but where ...

Rose was climbing down the ladder from the tree house and saw a weird marshmallow land! She was in a weird village, consequently, there were loads of people.

## COMMENTARY

Examining some of Theresa's vocabulary choices, the choice of 'swirling and spinning' is extremely effective, in part because of the alliteration, but also because these verbs are precise. The repetition, along with the modifying adverb 'gracefully', suggests that this movement continues for some time. However, the use of 'weird' twice in the following paragraph is less successful. There is no indication as to what is odd about the place, but even if the intention was to create a general effect without detail, a word such as 'strange' would work better. Similarly, 'loads' is too informal for a story; 'crowds' or 'huge numbers' would be more appropriate. Theresa's choice of adverbials is also less successful. 'Suddenly' is a reliable friend, but 'unexpectedly' is a little confusing – it might have been unexpected at that moment for Rose, but surely not an unexpected event in a tornado. 'Rapidly' also is a good word which, however, does not quite convey the right sense of speed in this context. 'Consequently' simply does not fit in the context in which Theresa uses it; she has perhaps misunderstood its meaning or is trying to suggest something about the village and its people which needs to be explained more clearly to be understood.

### Next steps for Theresa

Theresa would benefit from discussion of vocabulary choices, both in text she is reading, either whole class or in groups, and particularly in her own and other pupils' writing. Such discussion can begin with self-evaluation, where children identify words they feel work particularly well, and consider why the words are effective. They can then identify and discuss vocabulary choices that they were less happy with, and again think about why these did not work so well, and compare them with possible alternatives. At this point they may refer to a thesaurus, being careful to check that the alternatives do work in the context of their own writing. For example, alternatives to 'weird' include 'eerie', 'unearthly', 'ghostly', 'mysterious' and 'strange', but also 'abnormal', 'preternatural' and 'unusual'. Finally, they should try reading the work aloud to check that if words are repeated, the repetition enhances the writing rather than sounding clumsy and detracting from the overall effect. They can also listen for any alliteration or assonance which, although it may not have been intentional, may also enhance the impression the writing creates.

The third sample to be considered is also a fiction piece, this time from a year 6 boy. This sample was discussed in Chapter 6 in terms of its grammatical structure.

## CHILDREN'S WRITING

Morgan, year 6: Rainforest description: draft

*As I turned the corner I see a lovely stream with rocks covered in thick green moss beside it. I walked on, a huge bromeliad stopped me in my path. Hanging by the bromeliad there are vines handing lifelessly on the branch. The air was humid, As I approach the next corner I see cotton white fog. On one of the mossy rocks I see a bright green slightly-camoflouge millipede slithering across the soft moss. On my right I see tall towering trees with furry leaves surrounding the bare tree alone. giving it a warm coat.*

## COMMENTARY

Here we can see an older writer whose vocabulary is much more extensive and whose word choices seem to be much more considered. 'Bromeliad', for example, is a word that many adults would not know, while Morgan uses a number of adjectives to create a picture of his setting: 'thick green moss', 'tall towering trees', the 'humid' air. He tried to be precise in his description: the millipede is not simply 'bright green', but the colour makes it 'slightly camouflaged', with the careful use of the modifier 'slightly'. His images are thoughtfully constructed: the vines are living plants, but the way they hang over a branch is described as lifeless; the furry leaves give trees warm coats; the fog is the colour of cotton, suggesting a bright white rather than a greyish one.

## *Next steps for Morgan*

As was the case for Theresa, discussion of word choices and reading aloud are the key to further improvement. Morgan might, for example, on reading his piece through have noticed the repetition of 'moss' and 'hanging', and considered the impact of that repetition.

Children are often encouraged to think of alternatives to the word 'said' to use in reporting clauses. This can be challenging, as the following extract from a story shows. Mariette did not start a new line for each piece of direct speech, but that has been done here to make her vocabulary choices clearer. The full story can be seen in Chapter 3.

## CHILDREN'S WRITING

Mariette, year 3: Story

"Hey" said a plant.

"What" I replied.

"Why are you here?" arnsward the plant.

"I own the shop"

"Hey! Wait a minite you're a plant"

"Ahh" I interrrupted "Get away from my shop."

"Wait! I'm good, all I want here is to get out."

"But I don't know how to?" shouted the plant.

"What's happening here?" I asked.

"I belive the Quween (vilot) is hungry and wants food!" Arnsward, the plant.

changing the subject I delitfully asked "What's your name"

## COMMENTARY

Mariette has used five verbs as alternatives to 'said' (replied, answered, interrupted, shouted, asked), and has modified one with an adverb ('delightfully'). The variety does add interest to the writing and 'interrrupted' is a particularly effective verb. However, her choices are not always appropriate: she uses 'answered' in relation to a question and though it is, of course, possible to answer a question with a question, it is perhaps not a successful choice here; later on her choice of 'delightfully' to modify 'asked' is puzzling.

### Next steps for Mariette

Once again, review and redrafting are the keys to improving Mariette's vocabulary choices. Providing a bank of alternatives to 'said' can be useful, but children need to select carefully and critically to ensure that the words chosen are used appropriately and effectively. They also need to know that there is nothing wrong with 'said', and that sometimes it is the best choice, and also that adding an adverb or adverbial phrase might work better than changing the verb.

In the context of non-fiction writing, there are rather different criteria for vocabulary choice. First, good non-fiction writing is usually concise. Every word has to earn its place in the writing. Second, there is often a need for subject-specific vocabulary. Third, description is likely to involve accurate rather than striking vocabulary choices.

These characteristics are evident in the following sample: extracts from what was a long piece (first encountered in Chapter 4) have been included here.

## CHILDREN'S WRITING

Malia, year 5: From reservoir to tap

> Then the water gets sived again, and gets colleted in Eccup reservoir. This process is called screening. Eventually, the water won't have any wildlife or debree in it and it can go on to the next stage.
>
> Next, the water gets transported to the flash mixers where the water, and the bad things (baddies) get mixed together. Allum and sulphur dioxide gets added to the water to attract the baddies. There are 3 flash mixers that spin very fast to mix the water. Then, the water heads into the flocculator where flocc starts to form. Flocc is made of Peat, Algi, Bacteria, Cyclops, Water flea, Daphnia, and Protasia. After that the water reaches the dissolved air flotation tank.

## COMMENTARY

This writing followed a visit to the water-treatment plant and Malia used notes made in her geography book as a basis for this explanation. She has not simply copied the specialist vocabulary, as her spelling of words such as debris and algae show; she heard the words used during the visit and recorded her own notes. She gives an explicit definition of one term, screening – a feature of such writing. The use of 'baddies' is interesting as this appears out of place in this work and it is probable that the guide at the treatment works used it. Malia first puts it in brackets as a way of indicating that she intends to use this non-specialist term later. The whole text contains very few adjectives: 'different reservoirs'; 'compressed plastic'; 'the water is completely clean'. Adverbs are even rarer, with 'fast' the only example.

## Next steps for Malia

Malia has handled a significant number of new words in the whole piece, accurately and with confidence. In terms of her non-fiction writing, a focus now on a slightly more formal tone to match the specialised vocabulary would be appropriate. For example, she could remove contractions such as 'won't' and the more informal expressions 'gets transported', 'get mixed' and 'get added'. Using 'is' or 'are' ('is transported', 'are mixed') instead of 'gets' and 'get' is also a vocabulary choice, and will enhance her writing.

In using subject-specific vocabulary that children have learned in the context of a particular topic, they need to recognise which words are likely to be known quite widely and which may need explanation. This involves a careful consideration of their intended audience, but children also rely on their information sources where a decision has already been made about which words should be explained. The following extract from a piece of writing on homes through the ages, seen first in Chapter 4, shows a year 4 writer making choices about which words to define and drawing on her sources to help her with this.

---

## CHILDREN'S WRITING

Tiffany, year 4: Homes through the ages

Interestingly, tudor homes had jettys witch overhung the level bellow! Tudor homes were made out of wattle and daub. Wattle is weaved sticks and daub is a mixture of manure, mud, clay and sand that hardens when it drys. Tudors used limewash to make the walls white.

Here a partial definition of jetties has been given, but it is not clear exactly what they were. Wattle and daub are explained clearly, but the reader is left to work out what limewash is.

---

### Next steps for Tiffany

Tiffany could be encouraged to review the vocabulary she has used and reflect on which words she already knew before beginning to learn about Tudor houses and which she did not. This would help to establish which words might need definitions. She might also consider whether a glossary could be a better option than a number of in-text definitions. The answer is not clear-cut, as many readers prefer not to stop to consult a glossary even though they are left with only partial understanding, but these are decisions writers need to make.

## Supporting vocabulary development

Words are the raw materials of writing and children who have an extensive vocabulary have the materials to produce better writing. Vocabulary development can be supported through the following.

- Providing books that use more challenging vocabulary.

- During reading, identifying and discussing new vocabulary.

- When selecting words to focus on, choosing ones that can be used in a range of contexts rather than subject-specific ones.

- Having dictionaries to hand at all times so that looking words up to check meaning (rather than spelling) becomes a habit.

- Evaluating and discussing word choices with children, in relation both to what they read and their own writing.

- Encouraging adventurous word choices in poetry and fiction.

- Showing an interest in and enjoying words – their origins, precise meanings and sounds.

Of these strategies, the last is probably the most important. Teaching of vocabulary is difficult, as any words chosen may already be known by some children and may not be used in their independent writing by others. Children's vocabulary develops extremely quickly in the early years, with an estimate that on average they are learning 3.6 new words a day between 2 years 6 months and 6 years, and 12 words a day between 8 and 10 years (Saxton, 2017), yet much of this happens without explicit teaching. Some techniques such as the provision of word banks for lower attaining writers do not seem to have a clear purpose: if the intention is that they have access to key vocabulary for a writing task, this would be better achieved by discussion of the topic, so that they hear the vocabulary used in context; if the intention is simply to provide spellings, then copying will not improve their spelling and they are not being encouraged to think for themselves about how the words are spelled. The sort of displays of vocabulary sometimes seen in classrooms – Amazing Adjectives! Vital Verbs! – are unlikely to provide meaningful options for the many and varied writing tasks children undertake. Teachers who are themselves interested in words and who model such interest, are more likely to develop a love of language in their pupils. A teaching assistant in a year 2 class described how one year the children often chose to read dictionaries; it was difficult to know what led to such an interest, but it is likely that one or two children started the dictionary browsing habit, and that others then followed suit and discovered the magic of words. The development of this interest should not be left to chance.

# References

Hart, B and Risley, TR (1995) *Meaningful Differences in the Everyday Experiences of Young American Children*. Baltimore, MD: Paul H Brookes.

Olinghouse, NG and Wilson, J (2013) The Relationship between Vocabulary and Writing Quality in Three Genres. *Reading and Writing, 26*: 45–65.

Saxton, M (2017) *Child Language Acquisition and Development*. London: Sage.

# 8
# PUNCTUATION

## IN THIS CHAPTER

This chapter consider the teaching and assessment of punctuation: why it matters, why it can be hard for some children to understand and how it can be assessed.

Punctuation appears to be a priority for writing in many classrooms. Children are given many reminders and exhortations about basic punctuation and many individual targets focus on this aspect of writing: 'Remember your capital letters and full stops'; 'Try to use semi-colons in your writing'. If this emphasis on punctuation were successful, all children by the end of the primary years would be punctuating accurately, using a wide range of punctuation and making stylistic choices in terms of their punctuation. Indeed, many are, but others continue to make basic mistakes in terms of, for example, punctuating sentence boundaries and using apostrophes – as, of course, do many adults. The huge success of Lynne Truss's book, *Eats, Shoots and Leaves* (2003), a best-seller in the early years of this century, is testament to our continuing interest in, and struggle with, punctuation. However, Hall (2001) suggests that teachers tend to emphasise naming punctuation marks and teaching rules for their use, rather than giving explanations of them, and that children often can recite the rule but are not able to apply it in their own writing. Hall (2009) cites Sing (2006), who found that while children could often make the right choices for use of apostrophes, they did not always have a good understanding of the reason for the choice, and that many children still had misconceptions about the function of apostrophes.

If we are to understand why some children find it so difficult to grasp punctuation, we need to assess not only their use of it in their writing, but also their understanding of it through discussion. Consider, for example, this conversation with Georgina, aged 9.

Adult:      Can you tell me what full stops are for?

Georgina:   They're so you can have a breath at the end of a sentence.

Adult:      So what are commas for?

Georgina:   They're for children with asthma, who need a breath in the middle of the sentence.

Here, a popular explanation of punctuation given to children – that it is to do with breathing or pausing rather than grammatical boundaries – has led Georgina to hypothesise an explanation for commas which may then cause her difficulties when she thinks about them being used in lists or to separate short phrases or even single words. The following example demonstrates this:

Later on, however, the travellers, undeterred, continued their journey.

Not even a child with severe asthma is likely to need four breaths while reading that sentence aloud, and pausing four times would also sound very odd. Hall (2001) indicates that explanations of punctuation that focus on how to read texts aloud are not helpful. Punctuation is not a form of stage direction; it is there to clarify meaning.

The National Curriculum programme of study (DfE, 2013) gives a clear picture of expectations for punctuation from year 1 to year 6.

Year 1 pupils should be:

- beginning to punctuate sentences using a capital letter and a full stop, question mark or exclamation mark;

- using a capital letter for names of people, places, the days of the week, and the personal pronoun 'I'.

Year 2 pupils should be:

- learning how to use both familiar and new punctuation correctly, incuding full stops, capital letters, exclamation marks, question marks, commas for lists and apostrophes for contracted forms and the possessive (singular).

Year 3 and 4 pupils should be:

- using commas after fronted adverbials;

- indicating possession by using the possessive apostrophe with plural nouns.

Year 5 and 6 pupils should be:

- using commas to clarify meaning or avoid ambiguity in writing;

- using hyphens to avoid ambiguity;

- using brackets, dashes or commas to indicate parenthesis;

- using semi-colons, colons or dashes to mark boundaries between independent clauses;

- using colons to introduce a list;

- punctuating bullet points consistently.

---
## IN THE CLASSROOM

The teacher assessment frameworks for 2018 to 2019 (Standards and Testing Agency, 2017) have the following references to punctuation.

**Key Stage 1**

| Working towards the expected standard | Demarcate some sentences with capital letters and full stops. |
|---|---|
| Working at the expected standard | Demarcate most sentences in their writing with capital letters and full stops, and use question marks correctly when required. |
| Working at greater depth within the expected standard | Use the punctuation taught at Key Stage 1 mostly correctly. |

**Key Stage 2**

| Working towards the expected standard | Use capital letters, full stops, question marks, commas for lists and apostrophes for contraction mostly accurately. |
|---|---|
| Working at the expected standard | Use the range of punctuation taught at Key Stage 2 mostly correctly (e.g. inverted commas and other punctuation to indicate direct speech). |
| Working at greater depth within the expected standard | Use the range of punctuation taught at Key Stage 2 correctly (e.g. semi-colons, dashes, colons, hyphens) and, when necessary, use such punctuation precisely to enhance meaning and avoid ambiguity. |

---

The programme of study and guidance on assessment of this aspect of writing are clearly more detailed and specific than for other aspects, making assessment of punctuation relatively straightforward. There are, however, some points to consider before beginning the process. The first is that punctuation can usually be divided into necessary, rule-based punctuation that is either right or wrong, and punctuation that is optional or where there are choices, which is more a question of style. An example of the first type is the use of apostrophes, while an example of the second type is the use (as suggested in the programme of study for year 6) of alternative ways to mark some clause boundaries. Indeed, there is some flexibility in the use of commas, with the so-called Oxford comma being an example. (This is the inclusion of a comma before the conjunction and final item in a list – for example, 'You will need eggs, broccoli, and tomatoes.') Even the use of capital letters for names is not at all straightforward in many instances – for example, key stage used to be capitalised in government publications, but this is no longer the case. It is important that children understand the distinction between 'right or wrong' punctuation and 'you choose' punctuation, particularly as we are more likely to engage with anything where we feel we have some freedom. The aim is that children punctuate accurately as required, but also use the 'optional' punctuation to enhance their writing.

The second important point is that the statutory requirements and guidance on punctuation are based on an assumption that children can recognise grammatical boundaries such as clause and sentence boundaries. But it is not necessarily the case that children do recognise these boundaries: in Liam's story, seen first in Chapter 3, even noun phrases are not recognised as grammatical units, as his use of commas in a list shows:

he saw the children the, rabbit the, cat the, dog the, pig, the chikens the, calf

Explanations might be considered as a way of addressing this issue, but it is hard to find explanations of grammatical units that make sense to children (or even, indeed, to some adults). A definition of a sentence will not help those who find it difficult to recognise sentences (Hall and Robinson, 1996). Children need to come to a sense of what is and is not a sentence – or a clause or phrase – through a range of experiences and through hearing the terminology used in many contexts. They need to develop an awareness of when a sentence is incomplete – for example, when there is no verb – or when two or more sentences have been joined together by a comma (the so-called comma splice), rather than the boundary being demarcated by a full stop, or a semi-colon. It is also important to note that, as discussed in the last chapter, sometimes sentences are muddled and need to be restructured, and until this has been remedied it is not possible to proofread for punctuation errors, as the example which follows demonstrates.

## CHILDREN'S WRITING

Edward, year 1: Description of a setting

long. dry, grass and. gooey mud it's sticky! A soft like a pillow and bumpy, brown barck. super Crunchy leves like dinosors bashing thir teeth and owls hooting. Nosey thing left righ foweds backweds and bilow.

## COMMENTARY

The writer has not successfully moved from ideas and phrases to full sentences, perhaps because he was so keen to try to demonstrate all the success criteria he had been given, which included using commas in a list of adjectives and using a simile, or perhaps because he felt that a description was a form of writing which did not require verbs. As he has not written in sentences it is not possible to demarcate sentence boundaries in any meaningful way.

## Next steps for Edward

Edward needs support in reading his writing through, not to check for punctuation in the first place, but to check for sense. Children can quickly be discouraged when they try to read their own work and cannot make sense of it, and adult assistance in salvaging the writing, adding missing words and phrases, reorganising sentences and constantly rereading until a coherent piece has been produced, can be vital.

Compare Edward's piece of ambitious but ultimately unsuccessful writing with a much simpler piece from another child in Key Stage 1.

## CHILDREN'S WRITING

Rosie, year 2: All about me

My name is Rosie.

I have yellow hair.

I have blue eyes.

I have blue hair ties.

I have white hair slides.

I have yellow eyelashes.

I have three sisters.

one called Morag

(she is the oldest)

the next is Jemima

the last is Geraldine

(she is the yongest)

and I have a

mummy and daddy.

## COMMENTARY

Because the first part of the piece is in short, simple, repetitive sentences it is easy for the child to recognise sentence boundaries. This is also helped by the way she has started each sentence on a new line. However, in the second part, where the sentence structure becomes more complex, punctuation is less accurate; Rosie does, though, demonstrate her interest in punctuation by successfully using brackets to include additional pieces of information. Since these had not been taught, she must have noticed them when reading and independently worked out their purpose. This interest in punctuation and confidence to experiment with it is important.

### Next steps for Rosie

Although the punctuation is not complete in this piece, Rosie is probably not ready to consider more accurate punctuation for the last, extended, sentence, and indeed adults might not agree on how best to punctuate it. A more useful focus would be combining some of the short, simple sentences.

Consistent demarcation of sentence boundaries often takes time to achieve, and indeed children throughout Key Stage 2 may not always remember it, particularly when they are focusing on other aspects of writing. Compare these two samples from the same child in the summer term of year 1.

## CHILDREN'S WRITING

Ana, year 1

On saturday Kathryn came for a sleepover. At the sleepover we had lots of fun. First we went to the kids mueseam! Next we went to see the cars in the garede there was lots of things to learn! Last we went to have a story at the story center! Finely we wnet to see zoom the robot we played zoom ses. Then we went to the out side play area.

## COMMENTARY

There are nine sentences in this work, with eight boundaries; the child has demarcated six of these, using three exclamation marks and three full stops, and starting all six following sentences with capital letters.

## CHILDREN'S WRITING

Ana, year 1: The magic door

Once upon a time there was a little girl called Ana. she always wanted to go on an adventure. one day she found a rondom old door just silltng there Ana steped inside all there was is the othor side of her bedroom she stepd in it and the adventure began. In the door was the most dark and goomest forest. Ana had ever seen. she had a wonder arownd until she was lost ohno Ana said im loist I need to get home. she sow a creauture. she took a photo then there was more oh she said hello little guy she said now I had to find a way home she thout. then she found a cave she went inside it was dar. It is good she had a torch she turnd it on and she chouod see a huge bear! runnnnn!!! she shouted she ran as fast as she chould the bear was calcing up and she chould see the door she leped in and locked he door phew Ana said I am never going there again. she said. The end.

This piece, first seen in Chapter 3, consists of an impressive 24 sentences, with 23 boundaries to mark. (Analysis is somewhat complicated by the use of direct speech.) She has demarcated one sentence boundary with both a full stop and a capital letter, but has also punctuated a non-boundary in this way on the fourth line, between *forest* and *Ana*. She has punctuated eight boundaries with a full stop but no capital letter, and fourteen boundaries are not punctuated. Compared with the

75 per cent success rate in the first sample, this is a much lower rate, but this is hardly surprising. A recount of an experience is easier to write than an invented story, and until punctuation becomes automatic, trying to remember it places an additional strain on the writer. This has more impact on longer pieces where writing stamina is called for. Ana's attention was absorbed by the excitement of her story and the need to create tension and to manage her plot. The programme of study recognises that punctuation should not be at the forefront of the writer's mind during the composition stage by its repeated emphasis on proofreading for punctuation errors; the proofreading stage is the one where checking basic transcriptional aspects fits best. It is worth noting that Ana did make use of exclamation marks at the climax of the story and the three exclamation marks used together neatly parallel the repeated letters in *runnnnn.*

## Next steps for Ana

Simply asking a child to look back through their writing to check capital letters and full stops is not likely to prompt an enthusiastic response. It is often better to ask children to work in pairs, noting together where the sentence ends are and then checking for punctuation. This needs to be modelled briefly but regularly until the children are familiar with the process. Ana might also be interested to investigate the punctuation of direct speech in books, and may then wish to try this out in her own writing. Children should always be clear that the most important aspects of their writing are the compositional ones, and the checking of transcriptional elements such as spelling and punctuation are essentially tidying up activities, similar to tidying up the classroom – not thrilling but necessary.

As children move through Key Stages 1 and 2 they may be using a wider range of punctuation while at the same time still not using basic punctuation consistently. This is evident in Rhys's work, seen first in Chapter 4. (Square brackets indicate missing sentence boundary punctuation – either a missing full stop or missing full stop and capital letter.)

---

## CHILDREN'S WRITING

Rhys, year 4: Explanation

How the water cycle works

Do you know 70% of water is in the oceon. 90% of water is your brain [ ] Incredibul isn't it. And this is the water cycle works.

In the begining water is at the sea, and the sun comes out [ t]he trees rotts suck up the trunck and to the leves and up to the leaves and up into the air …

Next the water vapour is in the sky and it forms a cloud, this is called condensation [ ] while its up in the air it goyns to more cloudes [ ]

The clouds can't hold much longer so it rains and falls on montins and ether goes under ground or over ground [ i]t is called run-off or ground waterflow.

Last of all the water goes back to the sea. The water cycle goes on and on and never stops. 70% of water is in your body. To find out more information go to: 'facts of the water cycle' from profeser of the Word of wonders.

## COMMENTARY

Rhys has marked eight sentence boundaries but at two boundaries the full stop is missing and at three both full stop and capital letter. He has failed to use question marks at the end of the first and third sentences, and has used a comma splice between 'it forms a cloud' and 'this is called condensation'; a full stop or semi-colon is needed here. Rhys uses an apostrophe for contraction in 'can't' but not in 'it's'. He also uses ellipsis after 'air', a hyphen in run-off, a colon, quite appropriately, in the last sentence, and also inverted commas in the last sentence to mark a title. However, his use of capitals in 'professor of the Word of wonders' is a little erratic.

## Next steps for Rhys

Although Rhys is three years older than Ana, the basic proofreading process with a writing partner is still necessary. It will also allow Rhys to note other minor errors such as missing words, and he might also be challenged on some of his information about the water cycle. The checking of writing, as any writer will testify, covers all aspects of writing, since it is about how the writing will appear to the reader.

Many children do successfully master sentence punctuation during Key Stage 1 or early Key Stage 2, as is seen in George's story, first discussed in Chapter 3.

## CHILDREN'S WRITING

George, year 4: Why Rhino has a horn

We all know that Rhino is the owner of a magnificent horn, but did you know that there was a time when Rhino didn't have a horn and didn't charge. He looked rather like a big fat grey cow ...

One very hot day, Rhino went to the watering hole to have a drink. Earlyer that day us monkeys put glue on Rhino's head. Then Rhino suddenly saw that at the bottom of the water there was a pile of bones. This very big curved bone stuck onto his head! All of the animals tried and tried to pull the bone off, but they couldn't. It was stuck!

"Hey Rhino you don't look like a cow anymore!" shouted Giarffe from a mile away.

"Whatch this, as well!" Rhino shouted back. Then Rhino charged at a tree, consequently, the tree fell down! So there you are, that's how Rhino got his horn, and why I have a long tail, that's a whole other story.

## COMMENTARY

George demarcates sentence boundaries accurately, and also uses commas to mark boundaries between clauses and phrases – for example, separating clauses in the first sentence and marking off a fronted adverbial in the third sentence. The fourth sentence also begins with a fronted adverbial, but here George does not use a comma; whether this was a conscious choice or simply that he forgot this was an option is not known. George has punctuated direct speech accurately, and he makes use of exclamation marks both in the direct speech and in his narrative. He also uses ellipsis to lead from the introduction into the main part of the story. The positioning of the two exclamation marks in the direct speech shows that they were added later, suggesting that George proofread his work, identified the punctuation errors and rectified them. George is meeting the expectations for punctuation in year 4.

As children develop as writers, they may experiment with punctuation, as they do with other aspects of writing. In the following sample, a year 6 writer uses punctuation to help him convey a speaker's accent. He is rather more successful in this than in his choice of vocabulary for a speaker of the time of the *Titanic*.

---

## CHILDREN'S WRITING

Paul, year 6: Tragedy of the Titanic (extract)

Here is another witness account from 3rd class passenger Donald Cena, 55. "Aye, me was 'avin' a pint wiv me mates w'en da flippin' iceberg 'it. Dat's ma lives dosh gone. At least a got out, mind ye!"

---

Paul uses apostrophes to indicate missing letters to show the speaker dropping 'h's and pronouncing 'ing' endings as 'in'. This is a difficult technique but can enhance the portrayal of a character. Paul contrasts the speech of this passenger effectively with that of a doctor (presumably not travelling third class), whose language is much more formal and whose accent Paul does not indicate.

# Attitudes to punctuation

It is important that children feel free to experiment with punctuation, seeing it as a tool they can use in writing to create effects. Noting how this is done in the stories they read is a useful way of supporting this, as it is easy not to be aware of punctuation – indeed, if we do notice it, that probably indicates that it is not being used successfully. Discussion is also valuable, as it develops understanding of the purposes of punctuation as well as its effect: why, for example, do some writers prefer dashes for parenthesis while others are fond of brackets? Why do some writers use semi-colons frequently while others never use them? How long do items in a list need to be before they are separated by semi-colons rather than commas? How many exclamation marks are too many?

As with so many aspects of writing, generating interest and enjoyment can only benefit children's attitude to writing, and ultimately, the writing itself.

At the beginning of the chapter it was suggested that children's understanding of punctuation can be assessed through discussion as well as through assessment of their writing. This is helpful because children may avoid some punctuation marks because they do not understand them, or use them in some contexts – for example, colons to introduce a list – but not others – to introduce an example – because they are not aware of an alternative use. A year 2 pupil, for example, was able to give good definitions of the punctuation marks he used; he stated that the purpose of some punctuation was 'to stop the sentence – with a question mark, an exclamation mark, a full stop.' He mentioned also separating sentences. He talked too about 'commas – for breaking up words like theres. I don't know what the one on the bottom is but I don't use it. Exclamation mark – a shouting out one, it's interesting, we have to speak differently.' He had confused some terminology – apostrophes and commas, perhaps seeing them as 'top commas' and 'bottom commas' – but clearly understood the purpose of apostrophes for contraction.

Discussion also helps us to understand children's attitudes to punctuation. An 11-year-old, for example, said that she considered that punctuation was always right or wrong; she had no sense of being able to make choices. She said that she was sometimes unsure about what punctuation to use, even though she was able to explain the purpose of punctuation marks she did use quite clearly: a dash for 'adding a bit of extra information on'; a hyphen for 'combining two words'; a colon for the start of a list; 'apostrophes for belonging'. She did say that a semi-colon was an alternative to a comma, but that is an error made by many adult writers and might have arisen from her knowledge of the punctuation of lists. It appeared that although she was knowledgeable about punctuation she did not feel confident about using it and did not show a positive attitude to this aspect of writing. In contrast, an 8-year-old spoke with great enthusiasm and interest about the topic, even though she found it much more difficult to explain the purpose of different punctuation marks. In describing what punctuation she normally used, she stated: 'In stories I use colons, commas, brackets. I <u>always</u> use brackets; I love using brackets.' She mentioned her love of brackets more than once, suggesting that she would restructure a sentence to give herself an opportunity to use them. Even when she could not remember the name for a punctuation mark she was keen to talk about it, referring to 'flying commas – I forget the name' when discussing apostrophes. She stated that she thought punctuation was important, and tried to give examples showing two different functions: to clarify meaning, where she gave the example of punctuating direct speech, and suggesting how the text should be read, where she mentioned exclamation marks. In the same way, when discussing apostrophes she produced examples to try to illustrate the possessive apostrophe for both singular and plural nouns, and also contractions.

The two children, then, provide an interesting contrast, with the younger child demonstrating a genuine interest in punctuation and an awareness of her ability to make choices, and also an implicit understanding of how punctuation is used even though she cannot yet explain it clearly, while the older child, despite being able to explain the functions of punctuation marks much more successfully, appeared far less interested in the subject and showed no enthusiasm at all for it. To her, punctuation is simply one more thing to remember and one more possibility for mistakes.

# Punctuation difficulties

## IN THE CLASSROOM

Some of the common difficulties found in this area include the following.

- Missing or misplaced capital letters. Capital letters may be forgotten at the beginning of sentences or the beginnings of words. The conventions for the use of capital letters are quite complex: for example, doctor needs one when it is a title but not when it is a common noun. Some children also put capital letters in the middle of words, seemingly at random. It is important to check whether they can recognise matching lower case and upper case forms; again, this is not straightforward as some are identical in shape, differing only in size (e.g. c, o, s, x, z) or position on the line (P/p) while others have no visual similarity at all (A/a, D/d, H/h). It is also useful to know whether it is always the same letter or letters which they represent with a capital within words, or whether this is quite random.
- Inconsistent punctuation – for example, some questions completed with a question mark while others are not. This is best tackled when children read through their writing and check it.
- Incomplete punctuation, typically where a pair is needed: speech marks, or brackets, commas and dashes for parenthesis. This is usually simply a question of forgetfulness, again best checked for and picked up at the proofreading stage.

# Conclusion

Hall (2001) has some useful advice for teaching punctuation. For writers in the early stages, he suggests that children should be exposed to texts that do not have one sentence per page or per line, so they realise that sentence breaks may occur mid-line. This could be done during shared writing. He also recommends that from the start children should be expected to write at least two sentences, so they have a genuine reason to use a full stop and capital letter to demarcate the sentence break. General guidance is that the classroom environment should encourage children to notice punctuation and think about it, and that interest and discussion should be generated. When teaching a punctuation mark, teachers should use one explanation consistently. Although there is relatively little research into children's learning of punctuation, such an approach is considered to result in children using a wider range of punctuation, using it more often and using it more appropriately. Above all, however, teaching should encourage a confident attitude, interest in punctuation and willingness to explore and experiment with this aspect of writing.

# References

Department for Education (DfE) (2013) *The 2014 Primary National Curriculum in England*. Eastleigh: Shurville Publishing.

Hall, N (2001) *Getting Ready for Publication*. In Evans, J *The Writing Classroom*. London: David Fulton, pp. 143–5.

Hall, N (2009) Developing an Understanding of Punctuation. In Beard, R, Myhill, D, Riley, J and Nystrand, M (eds) *The Sage Handbook of Writing Development*. London: Sage, pp. 271–83.

Hall, N and Robinson, A (1996) *Learning About Punctuation*. Clevedon: Multilingual Matters.

Sing, S (2006) *Making Sense of the Apostrophe: Young Children's Explorations in the Word of Punctuation*. Manchester: PhD thesis, Manchester Metropolitan University.

Standards and Testing Agency (2017) *Teacher Assessment Frameworks at the End of Key Stage 1 and Key Stage 2 for 2018/19 Onwards*. London: Department for Education.

Truss, L (2003) *Eats, Shoots and Leaves: The Zero Tolerance Approach to Punctuation*. London: Profile Books.

# 9
# SPELLING

## IN THIS CHAPTER

This chapter tackles spelling: the challenges of learning to spell, of teaching spelling and of assessing children's learning to spot gaps and understand what support is needed to enable them to make progress.

## CHILDREN'S WRITING

My favrt fing to do is witing silubus. and I love using my brain. to wiet words to!.

[my favourite thing to do is writing syllables and I love using my brain to write words too!]

Mila, end of reception

Chapter 1 considered the huge breakthrough children make when they develop knowledge and understanding of the alphabetic code and therefore are able to write independently. Mila learned in her first year at school that graphemes (written symbols) represent sounds (phonemes) and that in order to convey meaning through writing, she needs to segment each word into its constituent phonemes, in sequence, and represent each with a grapheme that may consist of one, two or even three or more letters. This skill is fundamental to spelling, and even much older children – and adults – will use this strategy to spell words they are unfamiliar with. However, in order to develop knowledge of conventional orthography, or, in other words, the English spelling system, children need to develop, alongside this phonic strategy, a familiarity with the visual aspect of words and to relate this to meaning. Homophones, such a feature of the National Curriculum programme of study for spelling (DfE, 2013), are a good example of this. A young writer might be aware that a word could be written as 'pair', 'pear' or 'pare'; over time, the different meanings of the word need to be linked to the appropriate spelling. The system is complex and mastering it will take many years. Even at this early stage, however, Mila has moved beyond an approach of simply matching graphemes to phonemes, as her spelling of 'to', 'do', 'love', 'using' and 'words' demonstrates.

The Gentry developmental model (1982), referred to in Chapter 2, which suggests that spelling development moves through five stages, from pre-communicative to semi-phonetic, phonetic, transitional and finally conventional, has been widely used in considering children's spelling, but in practice there is often considerable overlap between the stages, with children learning conventional spellings of common exception words very early in their writing careers, for example. Mila provides a good example of this.

Assessing spelling is not simply a matter of noting that children have misspelled some words in their writing, or scored badly – or well – on a spelling test. Indeed, Peters and Smith (1993) state that the first focus, when considering spelling in children's independent writing, should be on the words they do know how to spell, rather than the ones they have not yet learned. Kress (2000) distinguishes between accurate spelling, where the child's attempt accurately represents the word as the child hears it, and correct spelling. A focus simply on correctness may affect attitude to spelling, which is significant in learning to spell. Confidence, willingness to attempt new words, an interest in words and independence in checking spelling, are all important to good progress in spelling. Purposeful assessment answers the question posed by Peters (1985) in her classic book *Spelling: Caught or Taught?*: Is this child on the way to becoming a good speller? To answer this, a different approach to assessment is needed. A diagnostic analysis of errors (and, of course, an analysis of words the child has spelled correctly) gives information about the strategies the child uses to spell unknown words, the words and spelling patterns that have been learned, and the understanding the child is developing of the English spelling system. For example, the phoneme /k/ can be represented by 'k', 'c', 'ck', 'ch' or 'cc'. Children come to understand that 'ck' is found at the end of words but not at the beginning. They learn that when 'c' is followed by 'a' or 'o' it represents /k/ but not when it is followed by 'e' or 'i'. This knowledge is demonstrated as they attempt to spell unknown words. Analysis may also show issues such as a child spelling a word different ways at different times, suggesting either experimentation or bewilderment; or a regular misspelling such as 'definate', suggesting that the word has been written in that way so often that it looks right to the writer. Mudd (1994) suggests that analysis may also suggest that a word has not been heard properly or is regularly mispronounced (an example being the common substitution of *been* for *being*) and also refers to perseveration, when a syllable in the word is repeated (for example, giving *develeloped* for developed), which may result from writers losing their place in the word as they write. This chapter will focus on the diagnostic analysis approach, which forms the basis for well-targeted and purposeful teaching of spelling.

# Beginning to spell

Returning to Mila, it is apparent that she has already begun to recognise some of the visual aspects of words, along with their sounds. This can be seen from systematic analysis of her spellings. Some approaches, such as the Centre for Language in Primary Education's Spelling Assessment Framework used by O'Sullivan and Thomas (2007) categorise spelling errors – for example, into phonetic or visual – but this can lead to difficulties where a child is using a combination of strategies to spell one word, or where the attempt does not seem to fit in any of the categories provided, so the following approach allows the adult to analyse without categorising.

## CHILDREN'S WRITING

| Target word | Child's attempt | Comments |
|---|---|---|
| my | my | Visual strategy used (using learned graphemes at this stage Mila would have written migh). |
| favourite | favrt | Phonic strategy used – all phonemes apart from unstressed vowels represented, though the use of 'a' to represent /ai/ could suggest visual memory of the word. |
| thing | fing | Mila has written this word as she says it, using a phonic strategy. |
| to | to | Mila has learned the spelling of this common exception word. |
| do | do | This is another common exception word and again a phonic strategy would have suggested representing it 'doo'. |
| is | is | Note that 's' here represents the /z/ phoneme, but children are unlikely to write 'iz': this again suggests a visual strategy. |
| writing | witing | Here Mila represents the first consonant as she says it, but note again the representation of the long vowel phoneme; at this stage, she has been taught to represent it with the grapheme 'igh', so here she is likely to be using a visual approach. |
| syllables | silubus | Again, Mila represents the word as she hears it; she is unlikely to have seen it written down. |
| and | and | This is a phonically regular word, so Mila would probably use this spelling whether she had seen the word written down or not. |
| I | I | This spelling is usually learned very early on. |
| love | love | This irregular spelling has been learned – Mila may have seen it written in greetings cards. |
| using | using | This is another learned spelling. |
| brain | brain | Mila's phonic knowledge would lead her to spell the word in this way, and again it is one she is unlikely to have seen often, if at all. |
| write | wiet | Again, Mila has represented the first consonant as she says it, but has chosen to represent the long vowel phoneme in a different way from before, and again this is not a grapheme she has been taught yet. |
| words | words | This is a learned spelling as the long vowel phoneme /ur/ is represented in an unusual way. |
| too | to | Mila has confused two common homophones/near homophones. ('To' is pronounced with a short vowel or a long one depending on what follows it.) Many much older writers make this error. |

## COMMENTARY

From this analysis it can be seen that Mila usually represents all the phonemes in the words she writes with appropriate graphemes and has worked out some phoneme-grapheme correspondences for herself. At the same time, she has been taught the spelling of some common exception words and also is using her visual memory to spell other words such as 'love' and 'words'. She has made a strong start to learning to spell, and this is reflected in the enjoyment and confidence she expresses. This positive attitude is important as it is likely to develop into an interest in words that will help Mila to master the complexities of the English spelling system. Children who are anxious about spelling are likely to choose less ambitious vocabulary and become disheartened by irregularities and odd spellings rather than fascinated by them.

### Next steps for Mila

As Mila moves into year 1, teaching will cover the different ways in which phonemes can be represented – for example, that the long vowel phoneme 'or' can be represented by 'aw', au', or even 'ough' or 'augh'. This presents a potential problem for the young writer. If there are several choices, or even only two, how can the child know which is the correct one? Teaching therefore needs to group words with the same spelling pattern, so that children associate the words, seeing, for example, 'could', 'would', 'should' and even 'mould' and 'shoulder' as part of the same word family. Spelling investigations can also help children to learn which is the most likely spelling of a phoneme in different contexts – in other words, the best bet strategy. An investigation of the long vowel phoneme /ai/ would show, for example, that where the phoneme is not at the end of the word, a split digraph is the best bet in every case except words ending with an 'n', where 'ai' is more common.

Teaching will also include common exception words, where Mila needs to focus on the 'tricky' part of the word, recognising that most words have some elements that are regular – for example, in 'once' the beginning of the word is the odd part, while the end follows a pattern found in words such as fence, since, dance and prance. The look–say–cover–write–check approach works well for learning these words. It is important that while Mila comes to understand that words are usually spelled in a particular way, and that she will over time come to learn these spellings, it is still important to have a go at words she does not know, and that if she follows the strategy of spelling them as they sound, others will be able to read what she has written. Where children focus too much on correct spellings, their writing can be inhibited in both vocabulary choice and length.

# Spelling development

Children's spelling development over time can be monitored to identify strategies used, developing knowledge of spelling patterns and any difficulties that may need to be addressed with interventions beyond the regular class teaching of spelling. A normal pattern of development can be seen in Andrew's spelling through his infant years.

## CHILDREN'S WRITING

<table>
<tr><td colspan="3">Andrew<br>Reception, autumn</td></tr>
<tr><th>Target word</th><th>Child's attempt</th><th>Comments</th></tr>
<tr><td>I</td><td>I</td><td>Learned common exception word</td></tr>
<tr><td>can</td><td>can</td><td>Phonically regular word</td></tr>
<tr><td>jump</td><td>jump</td><td>Regular word with adjacent consonants</td></tr>
<tr><td>run</td><td>rumn</td><td>Bizarre spelling, difficult to explain</td></tr>
<tr><td colspan="3">Reception, spring</td></tr>
<tr><td>fox</td><td>focs</td><td>Plausible phonemic representation of the word</td></tr>
<tr><td>has</td><td>has</td><td>Simple CVC (consonant vowel consonant) word</td></tr>
<tr><td>fluffy</td><td>flufe</td><td>Plausible phonemic representation</td></tr>
<tr><td>tail</td><td>taul</td><td>Andrew has used the grapheme 'a' to represent the long vowel, but also added the 'u' to represent the short vowel he can hear in the word. The spelling looks odd because we see 'au' as a digraph, but Andrew has segmented the word very carefully and represented each phoneme he hears.</td></tr>
<tr><td colspan="3">Reception, summer</td></tr>
<tr><td>golden</td><td>goatun</td><td>Andrew writes the word as he says it.</td></tr>
<tr><td>hair</td><td>her</td><td>Andrew chooses the wrong grapheme to represent the long vowel.</td></tr>
<tr><td>witch</td><td>wich</td><td>A plausible phonemic representation of the word.</td></tr>
<tr><td>wicked</td><td>wicid</td><td>A plausible phonemic representation of the word.</td></tr>
<tr><td>lock</td><td>loc</td><td>A plausible phonemic representation of the word.</td></tr>
<tr><td>tall</td><td>tol</td><td>A reasonable attempt at the long vowel, but not what Andrew has been taught.</td></tr>
<tr><td>tower</td><td>towure</td><td>Andrew has used the 'ure' grapheme as seen in words such as picture to represent the unstressed vowel phoneme at the end of the word.</td></tr>
<tr><td colspan="3">Year 1, autumn</td></tr>
<tr><td>they</td><td>vai</td><td>Common exception word</td></tr>
<tr><td>live</td><td>liv</td><td>Phonemic representation</td></tr>
<tr><td>little</td><td>littl</td><td>The double 't' suggests visual memory.</td></tr>
<tr><td>of</td><td>ov</td><td>Phonemic representation</td></tr>
<tr><td>look</td><td>luc</td><td>Phonemic representation of the word as pronounced in Andrew's regional accent.</td></tr>
<tr><td>appeared</td><td>a peeerd</td><td>An interesting way of representing the long vowel phoneme. Note that Andrew thinks there are two words here.</td></tr>
</table>

| Andrew | | |
|---|---|---|
| **Target word** | **Child's attempt** | **Comments** |
| **Year 1, spring** | | |
| very | verry | Andrew may be using analogy here – berry, merry, etc. |
| little | litlle | Andrew knows there is a double letter in the word, and he is now familiar with the 'le' ending as in apple, bottle, candle. |
| people | peppul | Andrew has not used an appropriate grapheme to represent the long vowel. |
| favourite | fouvrit | Andrew's visual memory has led to this spelling error. |
| with | whith | This overgeneralisation of the pattern learned for words such as when, why, what, wheel, white is a common error. |
| **Year 1, summer** | | |
| played | played | Andrew has learned the -ed ending for the past tense. |
| finally | finally | Andrew is using visual memory here. |
| through | froo | Here Andrew is producing a simple phonemic representation. |
| thought | thought | This shows that Andrew is familiar with the 'ough' spelling pattern, but presumably had not known that it was also used in 'through'. |
| moment | moument | Andrew perhaps feels that a single letter grapheme is not enough to represent the long vowel. |
| **Year 2, autumn** | | |
| wanted | wanted | Andrew has secured the -ed ending. |
| heard | heard | Visual memory has been used here. |
| tasted | taested | This is an unusual grapheme to represent the long vowel phoneme; it may have been taught or Andrew may have noticed it when reading. |
| knife | nighth | This suggests that Andrew mispronounces the word and has produced a visually odd spelling. |
| two | tow | This is a common misspelling; it appears more logical to children as they can hear a /w/ at the end of the word if it is followed by a vowel phoneme (e.g. 'two of you'). |
| **Year 2, spring** | | |
| when | when | Andrew is familiar with the 'wh' grapheme at the beginning of words. |
| with | whith | He is still making this mistake, as he was a year earlier. Once a misspelling has been over-learned, it can be difficult for the writer to recognise the error. |

*(Continued)*

(Continued)

| Andrew | | |
|---|---|---|
| **Target word** | **Child's attempt** | **Comments** |
| jumped | jump'd | This is an unusual approach to the past tense form, though it is seen sometimes in poetry. Andrew had secured the -ed ending months earlier, so is perhaps experimenting now. |
| there | their | These homophones are often confused. |
| knight | knight | Andrew shows that he knows the 'kn' grapheme, though earlier in the year he had not known that it was used in 'knife'. |
| **Year 2, summer** | | |
| favourite | faviroute | This attempt is closer to the correct spelling than the spring year 1 version, and again relies on visual memory, but Andrew has transposed the spellings of the two unstressed vowels. |
| dangerous | dangerous | Andrew is able to spell correctly some quite difficult words, such as these. They have not been explicitly taught; he is relying on his visual memory. |
| journey | journey | |
| soldiers | soldiers | |
| chef | cheff | This is an unusual spelling as it is a word borrowed from another language. |
| their | thier | Andrew is still making mistakes with some common exception words, though, as seen in spring, he can spell this word accurately. |

# COMMENTARY

Analysis of Andrew's spelling shows that in reception he has successfully learned to spell words as he hears them. This is his preferred strategy into year 1, but here we see clear evidence of a developing visual strategy alongside the phonic approach. His errors show that he is beginning to rely on his memory of what the word looks like; this may be a result of his improving reading – he simply has seen far more words written down, many of them over and over again – but also teaching of spelling, and encouragement to visualise words rather than simply hear them in his head. His learning can be seen in his developing understanding of rules such as the '-ed' ending for the past tense of verbs. The writer learns that whether the verb ending of the spoken word is /d/ as in rolled, /t/ as in 'kissed' or /i/ /d/ as in 'fitted', it is spelled in the same way. This is in part at least an understanding of morphology – that elements such as prefixes and suffixes carry meaning and that suffixes affect the root word in systematic ways. In fact, this understanding begins very early on: depending on the root word, the plural suffix 's' represents /s/ (as in cups) or /z/ (as in cubs), but children are very unlikely to use a 'z' in this context.

Year 1 spellings:

Autumn:     travald, needid, peeerd, a peuerd

Spring:      opend

Summer:     played, called, finished, turned, decaded [decided]

Year 2 spellings:

Autumn:     baked, hopped, asked, triked, dribbled, wanted, smelled, tasted, marched

Spring:      looked, jump'd, danced, live'd, stopped, starte'd

Summer:     pore'd, starte'd, started

This detailed list shows how Andrew has moved from representing the word ending as he hears it, with either a simple 'd' or 'id'. There are no examples of use of 't'. By the end of year 1, Andrew is using the 'ed' ending consistently, but part-way through year 2 he starts to experiment with the use of an apostrophe. As mentioned earlier, he might have seen this, where the 'e' has been omitted, but he also uses it with the 'e', perhaps because he has been learning about apostrophes for contraction but is not yet clear about their use.

Overall, by year 2 we can see that Andrew is not only using a visual approach much more consistently, but he is also spelling more accurately, including less common words. These will not have been taught; when reading, Andrew is subconsciously noting the spellings of words and remembering them. He is still making some errors with common exception words – for example, the there/their confusion.

### Next steps for Andrew

Andrew's spelling is developing well. He is unlikely to need any intervention beyond the spelling teaching which is a regular part of the classroom routine. He could perhaps be helped to clarify the there/their confusion by learning to associate there with here and where; the shared spelling pattern is supported by the linked meaning of the words. He could then think of 'their' as the 'other' one. It would be important not to introduce 'they're' until he is secure with the other two homophones, as presenting the three together is only likely to lead to more confusion.

# Spelling in Key Stage 2

For many children, by Key Stage 2 a visual strategy, underpinned by a secure knowledge of phonics and regular teaching, leads to good progress in spelling. Increasingly, they are able to make spelling choices based on what looks right. They are likely to know when they are not sure of a spelling, so they can check it later on. For some children, however, this development takes longer than for others. Consider, for example, this year 4 child's spelling errors.

## CHILDREN'S WRITING

Sally, year 4

| Target word | Attempt | Notes |
|---|---|---|
| material | matirial<br>matiral<br>matirtal<br>matrials | Sally tries all these ways of spelling the target word in the same piece of writing. Only one, interestingly the first, is phonically plausible, but note the 'al' ending: this, and the 'a' in the first syllable, suggest a visual approach as both are unstressed vowels that can be represented by a wide range of graphemes. |
| come | com | It is surprising that Sally does not yet know this common exception word, but the use of 'o' instead of 'u' suggests some visual memory of the word. |
| through | throw | This spelling may represent Sally's pronunciation of the word. |
| metal | metl | Sally has not represented the unstressed vowel phoneme. |
| properties | propertyes | Sally has partially succeeded in adding the plural ending; she has included the 'e' but forgotten to change the 'y' to 'i'. |
| describe | discrib | The long vowel has not been accurately represented here, although Sally does use split digraphs in other words. |
| plastic | plactic, plastic | This is a phonically regular word, but the error in the first version suggests that Sally has paid attention to the 'c' at the end of the word, where often 'ck' is used to represent the /k/ phoneme. |
| smooth<br>between | smoth<br>betwen | These are not plausible phonic representations of the long vowel phonemes. |
| stretched | streched | Sally has selected a plausible grapheme to represent the /ch/ phoneme, but it is not the correct one in this case. |
| investigate | investerget,<br>envestrgat,<br>investagate | Sally tries different versions of this polysyllabic word, getting progressively closer to the target. It would be important to confirm to her that trying different versions and considering which looks right is a good strategy to use – and it has worked well for her in this instance. |
| rethink<br>looking<br>dark | rethinck<br>loocking<br>darck | Sally is remembering that /k/ at the end of words is often represented by the grapheme /ck/. She is not yet aware that this happens when the /k/ follows a short vowel. |
| product | prouduct,<br>prodict | Although neither version is correct, Sally has the ending right in the first version and the start of the word right in the second. It is helpful for her to know that both attempts are close to the target, with only one letter wrong in each case. |
| people | poople | This looks odd and is not phonically plausible, but again it shows Sally using visual memory of the word, and again she is only one letter away from the correct version. |

| Target word | Attempt | Notes |
|---|---|---|
| environment | envioument | This is a good attempt at a polysyllabic word, with three of the vowel phonemes, including two of the unstressed ones, correctly spelled. Sally just needs to focus on the third syllable. She has not represented two consonant phonemes, and while the /n/ is often not articulated clearly, it is odd that she has omitted the /r/. |
| else | els | This is a phonic representation of the word. |
| reduce | reduce | Sally spells quite unusual words correctly on occasion; assessment should focus on correct spellings as well as errors. |
| means<br>made<br>safe | mens<br>mad<br>saf | These three common words are not spelled in a way that is phonically plausible, as the long vowel phonemes have not been represented by appropriate graphemes. |
| bridge | brideg | Sally has the right letters but not in the right order. |
| countries<br>properties | countrys<br>propertyes | She needs to learn the rules for pluralising words ending in 'y', but the second example suggests she has some familiarity with it. |
| recognise | recognis | This is a good attempt bearing in mind how the word is usually pronounced; Sally is using a visual strategy here. It is odd, though, that in this and the next example she does not use the split digraph. |
| create | creat | Sally is using visual memory here. |
| feature(s) | feateres,<br>fetature,<br>featres,<br>features | Again, this series of attempts shows Sally wrestling with a spelling, starting with the correct beginning, then wrong beginning but correct ending, before going back to the correct beginning and then finally putting all her knowledge together. |
| Wednesday | wensday | Sally has spelled this word as she pronounces it. |
| stripes<br>parade<br>frame<br>safety | straps<br>parad<br>fram<br>safty | As with earlier examples, Sally does not seem to be secure with spelling choices for long vowel phonemes, and in particular the use of split digraphs. |
| width | whidth, width | There seems to be an initial confusion with 'wh' words such as white and wheel, but then Sally corrects herself the next time she uses the word. |
| length | lenghth | It almost seems as if the extra 'h' she considered in the previous word is still in her mind here. |
| soldiers | soilders | Sally is relying on her visual memory of the word. |

*(Continued)*

(Continued)

| Target word | Attempt | Notes |
|---|---|---|
| whipped | wiped | Sally has not doubled the consonant to keep the vowel short. |
| what<br>why | wot<br>wy | Unlike the previous example of 'width', here the 'wh' grapheme is needed but Sally does not use it, even though these are words she will have read much more often than 'width'. |
| February | Februrary,<br>Februry | Again, each of these versions is only wrong by one letter. |
| recorded | recoded | The long vowel phoneme is not represented by an appropriate grapheme. |
| stops | stopes ('It stopes when the ground slopes up.') | It almost appears that Sally's mind is looking ahead to the later word when she makes this error. |
| bubbling | bubbuling | This is a plausible phonemic representation of the word, but it suggests that Sally is not familiar with the group of words (table, castle, bottle, etc.) which have an 'le' ending'. |

## COMMENTARY

While Sally does make a large number of errors, including in some very common words, and while her attempts are not always phonically plausible – for example, her representations of long vowel phonemes – she is using some very positive strategies in her spelling. It is clear from many of the errors that she is developing a visual memory for spellings, and this is particularly evident when she spells the same word in different ways in one piece of writing, as if she is trying out different versions until she finds one that looks right to her. This persistence is a good attribute, as is her willingness to use more unusual vocabulary and to have a go at spelling words rather than look them up during writing.

## *Next steps for Sally*

At this stage, Sally would benefit from an individualised spelling programme, rather than sets of words given to the whole class to learn. The words should be those that she uses most frequently, such as 'what' and 'why', or that share a common spelling pattern – e.g. split digraphs or the rules for pluralising words ending in 'y'. If she does not already do this, she needs to be taught to focus on the part of the word that is causing her difficulty, and it will be encouraging for her to see how much of most words she already spells correctly, and how often there is only one letter's difference between the target word and her version. It is important that she does not begin to see herself as a poor speller, but rather as a learner engaged in mastering a very complex system. Looking back at writing done in earlier years can be very encouraging for young writers, as it allows them to see how far they have already come.

# Spelling difficulties in Key Stage 2

Some children have much more significant difficulties with spelling throughout the primary years and beyond. This may be associated with problems learning to read, and reading may be slow and inaccurate. The year 5 pupil, Ellie, whose spelling errors are analysed below, was one such child. A selection of her errors from a short piece of writing have been categorised according to whether they suggest she was using a simple phonic strategy or visual memory, or whether it is difficult to see why she has spelled the word as she does – bizarre spellings.

| Phonic strategy | | Visual strategy | | Bizarre spelling | |
|---|---|---|---|---|---|
| target | attempt | target | attempt | target | attempt |
| when | wen | night | nihgt | pirates | prayters |
| dead | ded | suddenly | suddnley | adopted | adtitd |
| would | wud | saw | sowe | sisters | stars |
| scratty | scrate | walking | wallking | think | thisg |
| onion | uyn | said | siad | bottom | boht |
| | | clothes | cothes | pictures | pitue |

## COMMENTARY

The errors based on using a phonic strategy or a visual strategy are typical of younger writers, but the bizarre spellings are of much more concern.

## *Next steps for Ellie*

Ellie needs an individual spelling programme. In the first place she needs to secure the ability to segment words into phonemes, in order, and represent each with an appropriate grapheme. She also needs to learn to read the word back to check that she has actually written what she meant to write. To develop her visual strategies she needs to be supported in paying attention to the structure of words – for example, the -ly ending which she gets wrong in suddenly; this is a surprisingly common error. She needs to focus on learning common exception words and words she regularly gets wrong, as correcting these will make a significant difference to the number of mistakes in her writing. Ellie also needs to overlearn spellings, practising look–say–cover–write check on each word a number of times, even if she gets it right first time, and perhaps saying the letter names as she writes. The *ACE Spelling Dictionary* (Moseley, 2012) could be a very useful resource for her, as it allows children to look up words they cannot spell and therefore might not be able to find in a conventional dictionary – for example, if they expect to find 'sausage' beginning with 's' then 'o'. The dictionary also supports the learning of spelling, because the way it is organised reinforces common spelling patterns.

## Spelling tests

Spelling assessment can also include spelling test results, or scoring how many errors a child makes in, say, 100 words of independent writing. These may have some value, but so often a child will get a word right in a test and then get it wrong in independent writing, which has to be the ultimate test of spelling knowledge. There is also a question as to how useful it is for children to learn to spell words that they are very unlikely to use in their own writing. In addition, if the same weekly test is used for the whole class, some children will develop a view of themselves as poor spellers, as was suggested earlier in the chapter might happen to Sally, and this in itself can have a detrimental effect on progress. There is also a danger that the weekly spelling test replaces teaching rather than being a way of checking how effective the teaching has been. Sending spellings home delegates the responsibility for the teaching and learning of spelling to children and parents, who are not necessarily experts. Regular short teaching and practice sessions in class give many opportunities for informal assessment and avoid the anxiety that weekly tests generate in some children. Peters and Smith (1993) recommend an individual approach, in which children log words they have found difficult to spell, learn the spellings and test themselves or work in pairs to test each other. Mudd (1994) suggests that marking should involve underlining the part of the word which is wrong, rather than ticking or crossing, and not giving an overall score. Counting what proportion of words in a piece of writing are spelled wrong is an alternative approach to assessment, but it can be skewed by a repeated word spelled wrongly, or by the child's choice of adventurous or safe vocabulary. A child who deliberately avoids adventurous vocabulary because of anxieties about spelling cannot be considered a strong speller.

## Conclusion

Detailed analysis of individual children's spelling cannot be carried out on a regular basis, and indeed for many children may not need to be carried out at all, since experienced teachers will note from informal assessment those spelling patterns and common exception words which are causing difficulty. Indeed, self-assessment should play a large part in children's learning of spelling, with children themselves identifying words they find difficult and planning how to memorise them, whether by grouping them with a family of words with a similar spelling pattern, using the look–say–cover–write check method, or finding a mnemonic to help remember a particularly problematic spelling. However, it is important that teachers are able to judge whether the type of errors children are making are typical of their stage of development or unusual, and plan spelling teaching accordingly. Particularly when an older child is making a large number of worrying errors, an individual spelling programme may be needed, with brief daily practice sessions (Peters and Smith, 1993). What we should not expect is that children will not make any mistakes. While their vocabulary is growing rapidly, they will be using words they have not seen written down very often, if at all, and they therefore may not have internalised the spellings. Expecting children to check every word they are not sure of while writing slows them down and they may lose the thread of what they are saying. Checking spelling should take place after writing, and therefore errors will be recorded and can be analysed. Providing word banks, which encourage letter by letter spelling, does not help children to learn spellings; it is preferable to focus on the spelling of key vocabulary before the class begins a writing task, using a quick look–say–cover–write check activity. These approaches should help the vast majority of children to become competent and confident spellers.

---

## IN THE CLASSROOM

When assessing spelling, the following questions should be asked.

- Does the child produce plausible phonic representations of words they write?
- Does the child show evidence of using a visual approach to spelling?
- Does the child use learned spellings, of both common exception words and spelling patterns?
- Has the child internalised any incorrect spellings of high-frequency words?
- Does the child know and use different strategies for spelling unknown words, including spelling by analogy with known words, trying out alternative spellings to see which looks right and spelling the word the way it sounds?
- Does the child check back on spellings to see that when sounded out and blended they produce the target word?
- Does the child know and use a range of strategies for learning spellings, such as finding the problem part of the word, using look-say-cover-write-check, or learning a mnemonic?
- Is the child willing to try spelling unknown words and able to articulate the possible strategies that can be used?
- Is the child able to use a dictionary quickly and efficiently to check spellings?
- Does the child see him-/herself as a good or a poor speller?

---

# References

Department for Education (DfE) (2013) *The 2014 Primary National Curriculum in England*. Eastleigh: Shurville Publishing.

Gentry, JR (1982) An Analysis of Developmental Spelling in GYNS at WRK. *The Reading Teacher, 36*: 192–200.

Kress, G (2000) *Early Spelling: Between Convention and Creativity*. London: Routledge.

Moseley, D (2012) *ACE Spelling Dictionary* (4th edn). Nottingham: LDA.

Mudd, N (1994) *Effective Spelling: A Practical Guide for Teachers*. London: Hodder & Stoughton.

O'Sullivan, O and Thomas, A (2007) *Understanding Spelling*. Abingdon: Routledge.

Peters, ML (1985) *Spelling: Caught or Taught? (A New Look)*. London: Routledge & Kegan Paul.

Peters, ML and Smith, B (1993) *Spelling in Context: Strategies for Teachers and Learners*. Windsor: NFER-Nelson.

# 10
# HANDWRITING

## IN THIS CHAPTER

This chapter explores handwriting – asks 'does it matter?' and explores its place in the current curriculum. The chapter offers practical advice for assessing children's development in handwriting.

Does handwriting matter? For most adults it is only used for quick notes, lists and so on, and less and less so even for these informal purposes. Technology seems to be overtaking the debate, and even the issue as to whether children should be taught to type is becoming less relevant to modern ways of recording. However, in school, children still spend significant amounts of time producing handwritten work, so at the very least handwriting needs to be legible. Does it also need to be well formed, neat or even attractive? Speed is more crucial than appearance for most writers. Indeed, the National Curriculum programme of study (DfE, 2013) makes it clear that the main expectation is that handwriting should be legible and fluent, and eventually fast; although children are expected to join, it is suggested that this will not apply to all letters and that by the end of primary school, children will be making their own choices as to which letters to join. Statutory assessment guidance (Standards and Testing Agency, 2018) states that at the end of Key Stage 1, children should form letters in the correct direction, starting and finishing in the correct place, and of the correct size. In addition, those working at greater depth should join some letters with diagonal and horizontal strokes. At the end of Key Stage 2, handwriting should be legible when pupils are writing at speed. Legibility may seem almost too obvious to state, but teachers do have difficulty reading some pupils' work and this is reported as an issue in public examination marking (Adams, 2016). Quality of handwriting receives only one mention in all the government guidance, in the requirements for years 3 and 4, which state that pupils should be taught to *increase the legibility, consistency and quality of their handwriting* (DfE, 2013).

However, as long as children in school are still producing almost all their written work by hand, handwriting matters. Not only can slow handwriting prevent them from showing how much they know, poor handwriting can affect children's perceptions of their own work, and hence their motivation to write (Bearne and Reedy, 2018). It is discouraging to be faced, day after day, with writing that looks untidy, cramped or erratic, especially when adults may attribute this to a lack of effort or attention, rather than recognising that there may be good reasons for the child's handwriting difficulties. Similarly, adults may suggest that children are rushing their writing, without checking whether they are, in fact, writing much faster than their neater peers. Poor handwriting also has an impact on teachers' perceptions of the content of the writing; Feder and Majnemer (2007) report that even when the content is similar, studies show that handwriting difficulties have an adverse effect on marks. A child with a fluent, well-formed handwriting style simply produces work that looks better, and appearances do count for most of us. Peters (1985) also suggests that good handwriting is closely related to success in spelling.

Even if we could ignore these issues, there is an important reason to monitor children's handwriting development carefully. There are indications that automaticity in handwriting matters more than used to be recognised, because it frees the writer to attend to the other demands of writing (Medwell and Wray, 2014). Unlike a writer in the early stages of learning to write, mature writers do not need to focus consciously on letter formation, how to join letters, or how to space words. They can write legibly and at speed for long periods. They may be slowed temporarily by wondering about a spelling, but never by needing to think about whether an 'a' is formed in a clockwise or anti-clockwise direction. The programme of study reference to fluency may be intended as a reference to automaticity, but this needs to be made explicit in the teaching of writing. This chapter will consider how children's handwriting develops over time, what assessment needs to take account of, common handwriting difficulties and problems, and to what extent style is and should be an individual choice.

Chapter 2 proposed that in the Early Years Foundation Stage, the priorities for handwriting were to develop a good pencil grip, the ability to control a writing implement, and the ability to produce recognisable letter shapes using the correct movements. Children may have difficulties with these skills because they have had very little experience of mark-making before entering the Foundation Stage, or they may have more generalised difficulties with fine motor skills. Observation of the child while writing is essential.

# Assessing pencil grip and posture

As this photograph shows, young children may experiment with a range of grips, but if they develop a preference for an unorthodox grip, this may affect the speed of their writing and also may cause discomfort, particularly when writing for longer periods. Grips are sometimes described as dynamic; this means that the fingers move to control the writing implement rather than the hand and arm moving as a whole. Some teachers describe this as 'frog legs' because the movement of the thumb and first finger when writing are thought to resemble the legs of swimming frogs. In the preferred grip, the dynamic tripod grip, the thumb, index and middle fingers work together, with the pencil controlled by the thumb and index finger, and resting on the middle finger, allowing small, well-coordinated movements. Variations on this grip, seen in children with good handwriting, include the lateral tripod grip, where the thumb crosses over the pencil to the index finger side, so that it braces the pencil rather than controlling it; and the adapted tripod grip where the pencil is held between the index and middle fingers rather than between the thumb and index finger. The dynamic quadropod grip involves the pencil being controlled by thumb, index and middle fingers and resting on the fourth finger. Inefficient grips include the fisted grip seen above, and grips where the thumb is wrapped tightly around the pencil.

Also important to note is the child's posture when writing: in this instance it is clear that because the chair is too low for the table height, the child has raised his elbow to an uncomfortable angle. When writing, children should be able to place their feet flat on the floor, with knees, hips and elbows at right angles. Children who kneel on their chairs may be doing so because they are too small to be at a comfortable height for writing, and they should be provided with bigger chairs or lower tables.

Particular note should be taken of left-handed children, who may twist their hand round in the so-called 'left-handed claw' in order to try to see what they are writing, since a normal writing posture will mean that their hand covers what they have just written. They may also turn their paper round so that they are writing towards their body rather than parallel to it. Handwriting is more challenging for left-handed children, who have to push the writing implement rather than pull it, and it is important that this is recognised.

Observation should also take note of paper position to check that the paper is to the right of the central body line for a right-handed child, and to the left for a left-handed child, with the paper at a slight angle rather than parallel to the table edge.

When observing pencil grip, we should also check that the child holds the writing implement near the end but not at the very end, nor too far back, as both will affect pencil control. How tightly the pencil is gripped is also significant: too loosely, and control will be poor; too tightly, and the hand will soon become tired.

Deciding when to intervene to encourage a good tripod grip is a difficult issue for early years teachers. Intervention may make children less eager to engage in mark-making, but once a child has settled into an unorthodox grip, it can be extremely difficult to persuade them to change from what by then feels familiar and comfortable. Probably once formal teaching of letter formation begins, in the reception year, is the best time to try gentle but persistent encouragement of a more orthodox grip, possibly using any of the range of pencil grips or specially designed writing implements available for this purpose.

# Assessing letter formation

When assessing letter formation, the priority is that the movement is correct – in other words, that the letter is started at the right point and goes in the right direction, in a continuous movement (apart from a few letters such as t, f, x and possibly k where the writing implement may need to be

---

## CHILDREN'S WRITING

Julia, reception: I can run

---

lifted from the paper). Sassoon (2003) emphasises the importance of this, pointing out that incorrect movements, once established, are very difficult to change. Sometimes letter formation can be assessed from the written product, but a letter that appears to be correctly formed may turn out not to have been when the child is observed producing it. Consider the following sample, by a child at the end of her first term in reception.

## COMMENTARY

Julia has produced eight lower-case letters in this piece of writing. The letter 'c' appears to be well formed, but observation would be needed to ensure that Julia did start at the top with an anti-clockwise movement rather than at the bottom with a clockwise movement. The letter 'u' which appears twice also seems to be well formed, with the lighter exit stroke in the first example showing that this was the end of the letter rather than the beginning, and in the second example the slight gap between the upstroke and the second downstroke providing further evidence of this. The letter 'a' also appears twice, and while there is no evidence that it is not correctly formed, it is quite narrow. Julia might work on this letter by starting with a letter 'c'. The letter 'n' appears three times, and while the second and third appear to be correctly formed, in the first Julia has clearly forgotten her initial downstroke and has added it afterwards. This is also the case with the letter 'm', so Julia needs to continue to develop the movement of beginning with the downstroke. This should also help with the formation of 'r', which is the base letter of what is sometimes called the 'one-armed robot' group, which also includes 'n', 'h', 'b', 'k' and 'p'. The other letter Julia uses in this sample is a 'p', and while there is no indication of any issue with how it is formed it is too small to be sure of this.

In assessing this handwriting, it should also be noted that 'j' and 'p' do appear to have descenders, even though these do not descend below the line, and that the letters are of fairly even size with appropriately sized spaces between words. Observation would be necessary to confirm these judgements and also to check formation of other letters that have been taught.

## Next steps for Julia

Julia has made a good start: her handwriting is well controlled and legible. Depending on what has already been taught, an intervention focusing on the 'one-armed robot' letters which emphasises starting with the downstroke, then going back up and over, might be helpful at this point.

Where children in the early stages of writing development have not made as good progress as Julia, it is important that both gross and fine motor skills generally are given emphasis; many activities encourage both strength and flexibility in the hands, and mark-making generally will develop pencil control without children needing also to focus on the particular movements needed to write individual letters. Teaching letter formation in a logical sequence – for example, based on groups of letters with similar formation such as a clockwise or anti-clockwise movement, through regular and frequent short practice sessions, will form part of the reception class routine.

The next sample to be considered is from a child in year 1.

## CHILDREN'S WRITING

David, year 1: Christmas story

> Mary and Joseph travad to
> Bethlehem and they wher
> gout to have a babby soon
> When vey goe to Bethlehem
> they needid to sleep a
> innkeeper let ther them sleep
> ther that night they hat ther
> babby and a angel a
> peeerd at the shepherds
> camet to Jesus and then
> the angel a peeerd at the
> men wighs men and then
> the. Wighs men brort gifst.

## COMMENTARY

David has made good progress during his reception year, as this sample from the autumn of year 1 shows. A systematic analysis of letter formation would not normally be necessary unless there are significant concerns about handwriting, but it is included here to show how much more information about the child's writing can be gained than is usual from a quick look through.

| Letter | Appropriate size and shape | Joined |
|---|---|---|
| a | Yes | Yes, apart from first line where entry strokes have been omitted; diagonal joins. |
| b | Yes, clear ascender | Yes, in 'babby', which appears twice, and 'brort'. First 'b' in the word does not have an entry stroke. |
| c | Not curved at top (but only one example) | Yes, to following letter. |
| d | Yes, clear ascender | Yes, apart from first example. |
| e | Yes | Yes, after first two lines: in 'peeerd' the digraphs are formed as pairs of letters (ee, er) which are joined. |
| f | Yes | Yes, one example only – gifts. |

| Letter | Appropriate size and shape | Joined |
|---|---|---|
| g | Appropriate shape but descender not always correctly positioned (wighs) | Yes, but no entry stroke when at the beginning of a word (goin, got). |
| h | Yes | Yes, apart from in first few words, but no entry stroke at the beginning of a word (hat) |
| i | Yes | Mostly joined, both diagonal (needid) and horizontal (goin, wighs). |
| j | | |
| k | (only one example – innkeeper) | |
| l | Ascender sometimes short (angel) | Yes, after first two lines. |
| m | Yes but no entry stroke unless joined | Yes. |
| n | Sometimes omits downstroke (e.g. second 'and') | Yes, both diagonal (and) and horizontal (soon). |
| o | Yes | Yes, diagonal (to) and horizontal (soon). |
| p | No entry stroke unless joined; descender incorrectly positioned (sleep, shepherds) | Joined to preceding letter but not to following letter (shepherd, sleep, peeerd). |
| q | | |
| r | Yes | Yes. |
| s | Sometimes larger than other letters (sleep, Jesus); no entry stroke unless joined | Yes. |
| t | Usually appropriate size, better when joined, No entry stroke unless joined | Yes. |
| u | | |
| v | Yes; no entry stroke (vey) | Yes, to following letter. |
| w | Yes; no entry stroke | Yes, to following letter (when, wighs). |
| x | | |
| y | Yes; sometimes a little high (babby, they) | Yes, exit stroke included in first 'they'. |
| z | | |

The evidence shows that David's letters are generally well formed. He does not usually include an entry stroke unless the letters are joined; while the teaching of exit strokes is general, practice in teaching entry strokes varies from school to school. David joins the majority of his letters successfully, using both horizontal and diagonal joins. He tends either to join the whole word or not to join any letters in the word; the non-joined words are all at the beginning of the writing apart from 'innkeeper' in the middle and 'wighs' at the end. His letters are generally well sized, apart from 's', but he has a little difficulty with positioning letters with descenders – 'g', 'p', 'y'. The spaces between words are perhaps a little large.

The minor inconsistencies in David's handwriting are to be expected at this stage. It is important that he knows that his handwriting is good because it is clear and easy to read.

### Next steps for David

David might benefit from lined paper to help him position letters with descenders correctly. Observation of him writing would be useful to check aspects referred to earlier, such as posture, pencil grip and position, and also his speed of writing.

As children grow older, they may develop a more individual handwriting style. However, it is important that this does not slow their writing down or make it less legible. Sassoon (1983) refers to fashions in handwriting that spread particularly among older girls, often producing decorative but hard to read

---

## CHILDREN'S WRITING

Matthew, year 6: A Christmas tale

A christmas tale

I was outside the toy emporium where it all began, but first I should probably introduce myself. Hi, I'm Tom I'm 12 years old and I live with my Grandad (Jess), my dog (Abu) and my brother (Corran). We all live in a cold and dark bungalow. My mum and Dad dyed whilst I was a baby, in a car crash. and my grandma died of old age. So it's only us now. But now, back to the story, I was standing outside the toy shop, looking at all of the toys I really wanted. I asked my grandad if we could go in, but he said "no. I admit, I was a little disapointed, but I knew why. Many years ago a shop keeper died of old age. and rumour has it that his ghost haunts the place. As we walked back home I saw all of the little kids laughing beside their mum and Dad. It made me realise how much I missed my Mum and Dad. When we got home, Grandad put Christmas dinner on. Whilst me and Corran hugged the dog. After that we got ready for bed. Tomorrow so that brings me up to now. Right now I'm in bed writing this diary. Tommorow is the 25$^{th}$ of December (Christmas Day). I'm hoping that Santa will come tonight and leave presents in my Stockings. Tomorrow will be a magical day... hopefully.

---

writing. There is a tendency in some children to revert to printing, which does have an impact on speed as every time the writing implement is lifted from the paper, however momentary this is, writing is slowed. On the other hand, some joins are also quite laborious, or difficult, as with 'q', and it is a moot point whether it is quicker to cross 't's and dot 'i's as one goes, or return to them at the end of the word.

The sample from Matthew, year 6, on the opposite page, shows some reversion to printing.

## COMMENTARY

Matthew's writing is inconsistent; some words are fully joined while others are entirely printed; others have only some of the letters joined. There is no clear pattern as to which letters Matthew does join; for each letter there are examples of joining to preceding and following letters, and examples where the letter is not joined. In the last four lines, for example, the letter 'm' occurs nine times, twice at the beginning of the word and seven times within the word. Of these nine occurrences, only two are joined in 'come' and 'my': in 'come' the letter is formed conventionally, while in 'my' it does not have an entry stroke or even a downstroke. In the two occurrences of 'tomorrow', containing three letter 'm's, two appear to have exit strokes, although these do not join to the next letter. In seven of the nine letters the central downstroke does not reach the line. This amount of inconsistency is interesting as it suggests that a decision is being made about how to write each letter. This may only cause an infinitesimal delay in writing, but it is more difficult to reach a level of automaticity in writing if there is so much variation. There is slightly more joined script at the beginning than at the end, but even within the first sentence the word 'the' is printed. 'The' occurs eight times in the piece, and is not joined except, possibly, in the examples on the twelfth and sixteenth lines ('the place', 'the dog'). Here, because Matthew is joining to the middle of the 'e', the 'h' is poorly formed, with the second downstroke not reaching the line.

### Next steps for Matthew

Matthew is at an age when he may wish to adopt a more individual handwriting style, and indeed the programme of study (DfE, 2013) suggests that children may choose which letters to join and which to leave unjoined by this time. However, if this affects speed and legibility, children need to consider what their priorities should be. Probably the best approach is to discuss his handwriting with him, focusing not on appearance (except insofar as it may affect judgements made of him and his writing) but on speed.

# Handwriting difficulties

The following sample, which was previously discussed in Chapter 5, comes from a year 6 pupil with developmental coordination disorder. Her writing at this stage, despite effective and consistent teaching by the school, is still extremely slow and laborious. She is left-handed.

## CHILDREN'S WRITING

Faith, year 6

The midnight train

the midnight train comes in to site
Goes thorh tuned all eyes gleming
they all wont a letter but the
Midnight train goes on and on
but it must stop somewhere but
it does not stop one girl crying two
Boyes wouering if they could clive it
but the midnight train goes form
dusk till dawn and then stop at a
mist place and this is the End
of the midnight trayn

## COMMENTARY

Faith's letters are mostly well formed, although she writes both 'o' and 'g' in a clockwise direction. Letters are largely joined, unless the school's handwriting style does not do this – for example, 'g' is not joined to following letters. She is not fully consistent with her joining, though, even within the same word: 'stop' is fully joined twice but once she does not join the 's' to the 't'. Letters are generally quite consistent in size, with clear ascenders and descenders. There is some evidence of her difficulties in, for example, the formation of the 'm' in 'midnight' on the first line, where she seems to have had difficulty with the repeated arch, or with the 'i' in the following word where she has not returned to the line before joining to the next letter, and has failed to add the dot. Two words later she manages the 'in' join without difficulty. But observation of her during writing shows far more clearly that the process has not become automatic. She is still relying on a visual approach – looking at the letters as she writes them to produce the appropriate shape – rather than hand and eye working together, with the learned movements allowing the writing to be free and flowing. Mature writers can usually write quite legibly with their eyes closed; the hand movements have become so automatic that vision is not needed.

## Next steps for Faith

Faith would benefit from practising letter patterns on a surface that offers some resistance, such as a chalk board, so that she gets sensory feedback. She could also practise the letter patterns with her eyes closed so that she concentrates on the movement rather than the appearance of the patterns. Patterns, rather than general writing activities which necessarily involve random sequences of letters, could help her to develop more flowing movements.

# Other handwriting difficulties

Lower case b/d reversals, and less frequently reversals of other letters, often concern adults. While these are quite normal in beginning writers, if they persist through Key Stage 1, they should be addressed: Sassoon (1983) recommends using letter families to clarify, linking 'd' to 'c' and 'a', and 'b' to 'p'. Children are often taught to use their hands as a prompt: fingers are curled into the palm while thumbs stick up; the two fists are then put together to make a bed shape, with the left hand resembling a 'b' and the right hand a 'd'. Other issues can be pressure – either too light or too heavy. When pressure is too light, control of the writing implement is more difficult, and writing is often faint and spidery; when it is too heavy the hand can become tired more quickly. Resources are available from specialist suppliers such as pens that light up to indicate to the writer when the pressure is appropriate.

Where children do have difficulties with handwriting, an important part of assessment should be a discussion with them about what they find difficult. They could then be encouraged to try out some of the many resources available to see what might be of benefit to them – for example, a sloping writing support, paper with lines in threes to indicate how big ascenders and descenders should be, and specially designed pens and pencils or pencil grips.

A checklist can be a useful way of ensuring that all aspects of handwriting have been considered.

---

## IN THE CLASSROOM

Writing assessment checklist

- Does the child have an appropriate posture when writing (feet on the floor, paper at a slight angle, parallel to the writing arm)?
- Is a comfortable pencil grip used (tripod or similar, allowing good control, with grip neither too tight nor too loose)?

*(Continued)*

---

(Continued)

- Is pressure on the paper too hard or too light?
- Is pencil control good, with flowing movements?
- Does the child write at an acceptable speed, or significantly slower than others of the same age?
- Are all letters recognisable (lower case and upper case)?
- Are all letters correctly formed? Are any letters reversed?
- Are there appropriately sized spaces between letters and words?
- Are letter sizes consistent, with ascenders and descenders the size of small letters?
- Are letters consistent in slope (vertical, forward sloping or backward sloping)?
- Are letters joined appropriately?
- Is writing laid out appropriately on the page (e.g. starting and finishing near the edge of the paper)?

# Conclusion

While it is true that the importance of handwriting in adult life has significantly diminished, it is still important in school. It therefore matters that children develop a fast and legible style that frees them up to focus on writing composition. Indeed, Medwell and Wray (2008) point to research that shows that automaticity of handwriting is the best predictor of writing competence, and suggests that handwriting interventions can lead to improvements both in how much children write and also the quality of what they write. This indicates the need for early and effective teaching of handwriting, and assessment that identifies children with handwriting difficulties in order that additional support can be put in place.

# References

Adams, R (2016) Poor handwriting 'may hinder students' chances of exam success'. *The Guardian*, 22 August. Available at: www.theguardian.com/education/2016/aug/22/exam-markers-complain-about-students-blue-ink-scribbles (accessed 3 April 2018).

Bearne, E and Reedy, D (2018) *Teaching Primary English: Subject Knowledge and Classroom Practice.* Abingdon: Routledge.

Department for Education (DfE) (2013) *The 2014 Primary National Curriculum in England.* Eastleigh: Shurville Publishing.

Feder, KP and Majnemer, A (2007) Handwriting Development, Competency and Intervention. *Developmental Medicine and Child Neurology*, 49(4): 312–17.

Medwell, J and Wray, D (2008) Handwriting – A Forgotten Language Skill? *Language and Education*, *22*(1): 34–47.

Medwell, J and Wray, D (2014) Handwriting Automaticity: The Search for Performance Thresholds. *Language and Education, 28*(1): 34–51.

Peters, ML (1985) *Spelling: Caught or Taught? (A New Look)*. London: Routledge & Kegan Paul.

Sassoon, R (1983) *The Practical Guide to Children's Handwriting*. London: Thames & Hudson.

Sassoon, R (2003) *Handwriting* (2nd edn). London: Paul Chapman.

Standards and Testing Agency (2018) *Teacher Assessment Frameworks at the End of Key Stage 1 and Key Stage 2 for 2018/19 Onwards*. London: Department for Education.

# 11
# WRITING AT HOME

—— IN THIS CHAPTER ——

This chapter focuses on children's writing at home. It looks at the interplay between writing at home and in school, and explores why writing 'in school' can be different for children.

Robbie, age 9, had been in his room for a long time: his mother called upstairs to ask what he was doing. 'Writing my will,' came the reply. Unfortunately, the will itself did not survive, but the purpose was to ensure that a sibling that Robbie had just fallen out with would never inherit any of his worldly possessions. Children at home can write what they want, when they want; they often do it in private and it may never be read by anyone, or at least not by a critical audience looking for how many success criteria have been met, or offering 'steps to success' for future writing. Of course, their writing at home draws on a range of sources and is influenced by their knowledge about writing, and there is often an interplay between home writing and school writing. However, in this example it seems more likely that home was the source of Robbie's awareness of the purpose, if not the form, of wills, possibly gained from discussions he heard, but more probably drawn from his reading of fiction.

Children are often clear about why they prefer writing at home to writing at school. Harry, year 2, stated he preferred writing at home because 'I get to choose my own stories to write.' He added that he preferred factual writing, but here too the element of choice of subject was important. Laurel, year 3, explained 'I would say writing at home because at school you have to write what the teacher says.' For Laurel, story writing was her preferred form. 'I've wrote one song but mostly it's just stories. I love writing stories at home. I do it on Swallows and Amazons, that monkey, they're going down the lake, it crashes. I base it on lots of stories and put it in one.' Laurel was very conscious of the importance of reading in inspiring her writing: she explained that the source of her ideas for stories was 'just books. Which book shall I do? Got it! It could be like The Lion, The Witch and the Wardrobe, the people are going to go into a wardrobe or a magic door or something.' In her own writing, she had a clear sense of how she could not only take a key idea for a story, such as the portal in the CS Lewis story, as her inspiration, but also integrate material from a number of stories, as she did with the Arthur Ransome stories which had been read to her. Harry's writing also often drew heavily on his reading; he had been enthralled by a history of Britain, and then wrote a long history of the country he had invented as part of his interest in map-making, which had involved making maps of imaginary railway systems, road maps of imagined places and eventually a very detailed map of his country, somewhat confusingly called Cornwall. The history consists of eight chapters, each of which had an accompanying whole page illustration.

## CHILDREN'S WRITING

Harry, year 2: The Historey of Cornwall

*the Island was Made*

first there was an Earthqake in South America. But a very rear peple called Lymestore droped of from the Beack in the Earthqake By 1121 it had grown one sqare Mile. of rok and Larver over years it Became a swerling Place of Larver and rok and Palm Trees then a rok came swirling from space and setled on the sea then the Island was Nearly dun

*Leo and Ethens time*

By 3132 It had grown to the sise of the uk and the rok and larver was fading and Becomeing rokc ground peaple were starting to apier the two kings were called Leo and Ethen the locol triBes were called Menits goshars and Minipies.

*The invashon of Porchigal Spain and England*

In 4139 the English Spanish and Porchagese invaded the Island all sides ships were coming with Men with wepons and Made war the Fight took a year and by November Leo and Ether were killed

*Cornwall Becomes Cathlikc*

in 1530 the King who was called Sebastian. cathlikc the head of the Protestont chuch said Sedastian why are you turning the country cathlick. Sebastian said Because I'm cathlik Myself But I'm Protestestant said the vicar I marriyd your sister said sedastian and I want her Executed! he said louder so one one of Sebastians servants with the Queen handcufd got a axx. and just ass the ax hitt the Qeueen and the vicor there heads fell off.

*Paece at last!*

in 1658 the princess was made Queen her name was Anita she rulled well and Made evryone verry rich and verry happy after she Died people wore Black till they forgot why they were.

*The verry sad Queen*

Anitas daughter Mary grew up to Be a good Queen she Maried a Duke His Name was Peter-Langton they had a BaBy girl Named Margret in 7181 Buke Peter-Langton Died of a Deseese Because a Moskitoe Bit him when he was and Hunt [out hunting] Margret found Him Ded in Bed

*(Continued)*

(Continued)

with a Blangket over his head she ran out into the Garden and and told Marry they wept and wept til they could weep no More and Queen Marry was sad Fore the rest of her Life

*Queen MarGret*

altho Margret was sad. she thougt she would Marry. Sir Peter-Langtons Brothers sun. IN 1845 she Married Farley-Langton. In 1861 the Queen ANountst she was goaing to have a BaBy Boy she [named] him Geogevis

*King Geogevis the VII*

In 1936 Geogevis was crowned and Became King. he Made everyone happy But soon a Geogevis got a Desise called malaria he got verry Ill and in1948 a Mystry Happend his Kitchen

## COMMENTARY

The influences of Harry's reading are very clear, both in terms of content, with events obviously drawing on Tudor times (the Armada, religious tensions, executions) and also language ('they wept and wept till they could weep no more'). It is interesting that after the sustained effort needed to produce this history, which was written over the course of several days, Harry did not complete the story, moving on instead to a different project. When asked to, he did find the story and read it out, even making some minor corrections as he went, but his intense interest in the story had gone. Children's writing at home seems to be very much of the moment; as Jo in Louisa May Alcott's *Little Women* (1868) put it, *genius burns* – and then stops. We can see an odd contrast here: writing at home can be sustained because of the opportunity to write for long periods, but also can be fragmentary because children are able to abandon writing they are not happy with or which they lose interest in. A few months later Harry wrote the following sample, which demonstrates this fragmentary nature of writing.

## CHILDREN'S WRITING

Harry, year 2: Playscript

| | |
|---|---|
| *Servant* | "knock knock". |
| *Prince Fredderick* | "whos there"? |
| *Servant* | "it is me thy Dinner is here". PRISONER! |
| *Prince Fredderick* | WHAT! |

| | |
|---|---|
| *Servant * | CRASH ... |
| Prince Frederick* | YOU JUST droped my lunch! |
| *Servant * | Shut up! Prisoner Ahahaaa! |
| *Servant * | SLAM! |
| *Prince Fredderick* | Wait! |
| *Prince Fredderick* | I wish I was not Locked up in this cell. Anyway It's bed time. |
| *Naraitor | P |

## COMMENTARY

The sample demonstrates Harry's continuing interest in history, but on this occasion he lost interest relatively quickly, and never returned to the script.

The element of choice is very significant; after all, at home, children can simply choose not to write – but it is worth considering whether being offered more choices about their writing at school could improve motivation. Harry, when asked how he felt about writing at school, said, 'I just think: that's all right'. Yet in free time at school he often chose to write, as well as writing infrequently but at length at home. Some children, of course, do not choose to write at home. Sita, aged 11, said she preferred writing at home, but then added, with praiseworthy honesty, 'I don't really write at home.' In its annual survey of children's attitudes to literacy, The National Literacy Trust (Clark, 2018) found that 30 per cent of 8–11-year-olds only write when they have to.

Another consideration for children is what happens to their writing when it is finished (or when they stop writing: the two are not necessarily the same). In school, Harry said, 'Our teacher marks it then it goes in our books.' The use of the word 'marks' rather than 'reads' is interesting. Laurel explained that 'The books have to be collected in and our teacher marks it and we have to correct it.' Children tend not to mention their writing being read by other children; the teacher is the sole audience. Laurel stated, 'I would like it to just go in the tray and other people read it before the teacher marks it.' She did not like the idea of other children seeing the green and pink highlighter used to mark the writing, but was quite happy to think of other children reading her unmarked work. At home, children are unlikely to be subjected to systematic 'marking' of their writing, and indeed children can choose not to show their writing to anyone, as Laurel explained when asked about who read her home writing: 'Just Mum. Sometimes Dad. Sometimes they don't read them; I don't show them if I don't think it's good enough.' Harry also seemed uninterested in an audience for his home writing; he did not invite his parents to read his work, although they did and he knew they were interested in it. It appears that for some children the act of creating the writing is enough, and they do not seek out or need the approval of others. There is an interesting contrast here with school, where there is an assumption that all children need and want adult validation of their writing, and that positive feedback is vital. It is interesting to consider why some children are intrinsically motivated to write, and indeed may find formal feedback demotivating.

Another difference between writing at home and at school is that writing at home often goes unobserved. At school, teachers feel an obligation to scan the classroom constantly, noting children who appear to be off task and taking action swiftly to remedy the situation. At home, children may disappear into their bedrooms for long periods, as Robbie the will-writer did, or even if they are in a shared space the fact that they are quiet, busy and not making a mess means that adults may pay them very little attention. This can be helpful for the writing process, which for many writers is very much a private activity; children who put their arms protectively around their writing are essentially conveying that it is not yet ready to share, but at school this desire to keep the writing private, at least for a while, can be over-ridden by the adult need to monitor work, and indeed to intervene to teach at the point of writing. The child who likes to stop writing every now and again to think about what to say, or even just to have a little break before plunging in again, can do this at home. At school, there is too much concern about productivity and being 'on task' to allow us to be comfortable with a child staring out of the window for five minutes. It is likely, too, that there are fewer interruptions for the child writer at home; at school, not only are there perhaps interruptions of the daily routine, there are often interruptions by other children. The typical seating arrangement of the primary classroom, with a group of children facing each other, almost invites regular interaction. The prevalence of the mini-plenary can also mean that children have barely started their writing before they are being told to put their pencils down, and this may occur several times in a writing session. At home, children can write in the way that suits them best.

Teachers often work hard to ensure that children have a wide range of writing tasks, feeling that variety will promote engagement. Some text types, however, are seen as of particular importance, while others (such as Robbie's will) would be seen as inappropriate. Without such considerations, children at home produce a huge range of text types, as Laurel's room rules, which appeared on her bedroom door, show.

## CHILDREN'S WRITING

Laurel, year 3: ROOM Rules

• No people that have Disney dresses or big dresses;

Please book a slot below.

[Half-hourly time slots from 10am to 8pm, each in its own box, followed. Laurel herself had signed in for the first, perhaps as a model for others.]

1.   Please Knock!
     * * * * * *
2.   Say Password
3.   Do what you needed to do
4.   Leave and put time

# CHILDREN'S WRITING

Milly, reception: hymn

Syh sh ine sun Shine Shineqiiygg for Long please help hevgh £p £nqr mykes

qsSleepi høpørihl Wa

Sun shine sun shine shine all day for Long please help hevan father makes us sleep in dep orinj we

Laurel later relented and allowed her mother to enter the room to return clean laundry without signing in.

This range is clearly seen in writing produced by a 5-year-old girl, Milly, in the space of one month at home, which included lists, letters, books and a hymn, complete with music.

## COMMENTARY

The sample on p. 145 shows how even at this early stage of her writing development Milly knows about different text types and has an understanding of the varied purposes of writing, coupled with the skills and knowledge that allow her to encode her messages.

The influence of school on home writing is, of course, crucial. Not only is school the place where most children learn basic transcriptional skills, it is also a place where all children encounter a range of text types. Patience, a year 1 pupil, wrote a playscript to be read at bedtime, and it is difficult to imagine her encountering this text type anywhere but at school. The playscript was written on facing pages of a spiral-bound notebook, with her own lines on one side and her mother's on the other. The book could then be folded back so the speakers could sit opposite each other and read their own lines.

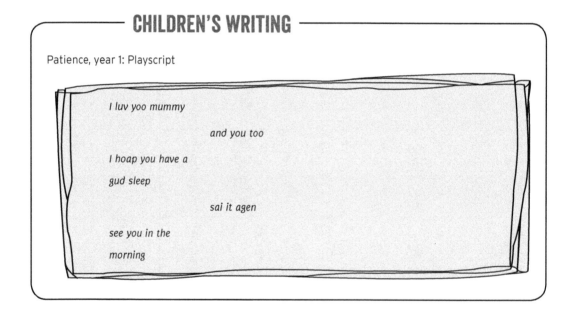

## CHILDREN'S WRITING

Patience, year 1: Playscript

*I luv yoo mummy*

*and you too*

*I hoap you have a*

*gud sleep*

*sai it agen*

*see you in the*

*morning*

## COMMENTARY

The notion of a script for such a well-rehearsed exchange is quite odd, but children have their own purposes for writing, and in this case it may be simply a desire to try out a form that Patience had been exposed to and was interested in. Once the reading had taken place and she could see that the script 'worked', she showed no interest in writing in this form again. An older child, Maya, also wrote a playscript at home, but this was intended for performance by her and her siblings.

## CHILDREN'S WRITING

Maya, year 4: Playscript - Robin Hood & Maid Marin

*Charicters*

Robin Hood Maid Marin frear tuck

little John Nacy Richard LH prudenece

Nacy Maid

Badys

Sheriof N Tony

2 Narators

*Script*

Narrator One day in middle of the woods Robin Hood bumped in to a stranger.

Robin I am Robin Hood who are you?

little J John my wife is Nacy she Just comeing

Nacy who is this?

little J this Robin Hood

Nacy I'll get the others. Bye.

## COMMENTARY

While the script is incomplete – indeed, the play has hardly begun – it demonstrates that Maya has knowledge of the form. She has listed her characters (although the division into good and bad characters appears to be her own idea) and she knows how to lay out the script itself, with the speaker's name given and then the speech. She makes use of narrators, as many playscripts used in primary schools do. Maya finds writing difficult, as her spelling suggests, but she chooses to write this piece because she has a clear purpose in mind – a performance to entertain her family. The characters she includes suggest that she knows the story well, and indeed may have seen a dramatised version – perhaps a film.

# Using technology for writing

While parents may be anxious about some aspects of their children's use of technology, they are likely to be pleased to see children composing texts on computers. For the children, word processing offers the opportunity to experiment with all the exciting possibilities offered by the keyboard, and learning to change the font, copy and paste and delete, and so on, as the next sample shows.

## CHILDREN'S WRITING

Erik, year 1: story

# A  familiar  world

There  was  once  a  boy  and  his  name  was  Peter,  he  loved  familiar  things.  He  went  for  a  walk  and  found  somthing  familiar,  he  loved it.  It  was  very  blue -ish .

He  took  it  home  did  rubing`s  with  it,  he  sckeched/drew  it.  He  thoght  it  was  butiul.

He  looked  at  all  the  familiar  things  he`d  found  they  ameadiatly  started  singing.

Then  dansing  then  screaming.  Peter  thoght  they  were  halerias.  Then they  started

to  be  familiar.  He  put  its  name  down  in  a  book.

**Part #2**--------------------------------------------------------------------------------

Peter went  to  bed  but  he  could  not  get  to  sleep.  Percy  I  can`t  get  to  sleep,  what

called  out  Percy.  I  (CAN  NOT)  get  to  sleep.  It  was  dawn  and  Percy

called  out  Peter  come  and  have  breakfast.

No i`m just doing a expererment

**Part #3**--------------------------------------------------------------------------------

Put  on  your  waistcoat  shirt & trousers;

*chapter 2*-----------------------------------------------------

**Soum- thing mustearias**

Percy  played  chess with  Peter  Pawson.  Mrs  Pawson  would  you  like  a  cup  of  tea .

**Part # 4**----------------------------------------------------------------

next    day

I    was    up    erly    &    there    was    early    silence    as
    I    heard    a    cackling        sound.
witches,    I    cried    help    HELP

*HELP.*

**Part # 5**-------------------------------------------------------------

Or

**chapter 3**

finally

the    end    of    my    tale

## COMMENTARY

Erik has clearly enjoyed changing font size, colour and type, and using symbols such as the hash mark, hyphens and slash mark. He did not use the computer to redraft his story; at 5 years old, the effort needed, and the editing skills, were beyond him. The story was written over several days, and this may be one reason for its somewhat disjointed quality and lack of a clear narrative thread. The one-word sections at the end suggest that he was keen to feel that he had finished the story, but was not able or prepared to write at any length by this stage.

# The power of writing

In some families, children learn quite early on that writing is powerful. Simply asking for Christmas presents is less likely to have a positive outcome than the traditional letter to Father Christmas. Parents who are excited and delighted to see their children mastering the skill of writing are more likely to be swayed by a written request than an oral one, and indeed there is a general feeling that issues need to be taken more seriously once they have been put in writing. Examples such as the following two show that even children in the early stages of learning to write will use their writing to affect their world – to complain, to request, to plead, and so on.

Mina knows that she can be rude to her parents in a way that would never be tolerated when she talks to them, because they will be so pleased to see her writing.

---

**CHILDREN'S WRITING**

Paddy, reception: letter of complaint

Jack was naatee He hit me

from Paddy

---

---

**CHILDREN'S WRITING**

Mina, year 1 (written on the computer)

Dad doonot pant [paint] the wall you ideat [idiot] mum stop beaing mean

---

# Homework

With the prevalence of regular homework for even the youngest children in school, inevitably some writing done at home is simply school writing delegated to parental managers. For families who value education highly, such writing may have more status than the children's own self-initiated writing, and indeed may be the only form of writing done regularly at home. Justin, a year 2 pupil, for example, talked about doing 'comprehensions' (a text extract with a list of questions to be answered in full sentences) and also about writing in a large notebook where he practised spellings and handwriting. Some of the practice was actually initiated by his mother rather than school, but writing at home was very much seen as being about improving his writing to meet school expectations. He commented that he preferred writing at home to writing at school because 'I can get my teddies out and cuddle them and Mummy helps me if it's tricky'. While he had a generally positive attitude to writing and was keen to show his work, his view of what was important about writing was a narrow one. He explained that he was a better (neater) writer than his father because his father did not practise. He considered that it was important to learn to write so that he could do spelling tests successfully. He did, however, have some idea about adult writing, mentioning keyboards and phones. It was interesting that he did not talk about the beautifully inscribed greetings cards he made for family members; for Justin, it appeared, this did not count as writing because it was not related to school tasks. Compared with other children, though, Justin did not really engage in his own writing at home, possibly because school-focused writing was such a priority in the family.

If both parents and schools seem to children to be preoccupied with transcriptional aspects of writing, children need to have a strongly independent view of what matters to focus on content and form in their self-initiated writing at home. Of course, mastering skills such as handwriting can be intrinsically motivating, but once mastered the motivation goes. Only composition can offer continual challenge to writers, and if children do not see this as mattering to adults, they are on their own with this – unless, of course, they have siblings who also write. The Brontë sisters are probably the most famous example of a family where children wrote for each other, creating a whole imaginary world (rather as Harry, who features earlier in the chapter, did with his younger brother).

# Encouraging writing at home

While we would not wish to pressurise children to write in their leisure time, it is stating the obvious to say both that frequent writing at home is likely to support writing development, and also that it is a reflection of a positive attitude to writing, which is also an important factor in improvement. Clark and Teravainen (2017) noted the clear relationship between enjoyment of writing and attainment. Teachers need to consider how they work with parents, but also how their own attitude and expectations may affect children's desire to write at home. Some parents may need to be encouraged to respond with interest and enthusiasm to their children's independent writing, and to provide a supply of materials readily accessible to the children. They may also need to be reassured that spelling and punctuation errors and imperfect handwriting are a part of learning to write, and that it is more important to focus on content. The story of a lonely and homesick child at boarding school whose letters home were corrected for spelling and punctuation by her mother and returned to her so she could see her mistakes is a poignant lesson in how not to respond to children's writing.

# Conclusion

Teachers need to consider how the classroom climate might encourage or discourage writing at home. Bearne (2002) suggests that children's views of their writing at home can be helpful to teachers in understanding how writing can be developed. It would be wrong to suggest that writing done at home is in some way superior to the often polished and inspired writing that may be produced at school. However, assessment of home writing may lead to useful reflection on classroom practice. Do children feel their writing is valued? Are writing tasks designed to be purposeful and pleasurable? Do pupils see themselves as members of a community of writers who support each other? Are they able to make choices about their writing and take ownership of it? Do their teachers seem to be interested in the writing they do outside school? Grainger *et al.* (2003) in a study of children's attitudes to writing suggested that children became less positive about writing in school as they grew older, but that there was more enthusiasm about writing at home, and they therefore recommended that teachers consider giving children more choice and independence in their writing to reflect the freedom of home writing.

# References

Alcott, LM (1868) *Little Women*. Boston, MA: Roberts Brothers.

Bearne (2002) *Making Progress in Writing*. London: RoutledgeFalmer.

Clark, C (2018) *Writing Enjoyment, Behaviours and Attitudes in 8 to 11 year olds in 2017/18*. London: National Literacy Trust.

Clark, C and Teravainen, A (2017) *Enjoyment of Writing and its Link to Wider Writing: Findings from our Annual Literacy Survey 2016*. London: National Literacy Trust.

Grainger, T, Goouch, K and Lambirth, A (2003) 'Playing the Game called Writing': Children's Views and Voices. *English in Education, 37*(2): 4–16.

# 12

# THE CURRICULUM AND STATUTORY ASSESSMENT

This chapter discusses the recent history of the national curriculum and statutory assessment of writing in England. While the curriculum changes relatively infrequently, it can be difficult to keep track of changes to statutory assessment and the detail of how it is managed, particularly when interim measures are in place, and minor changes are perhaps being made almost every year. But these details are important to teachers, as although minor they may have a significant effect on outcomes and therefore affect teaching. Indeed, they may even be reported by news media, in stories such as the 2017 one concerning semi-colons in the Key Stage 2 grammar, punctuation and spelling test (Sellgren, 2017), where guidance was given as to the acceptable size and positioning of the mark. The implication is that it is ludicrous to place such weight on tiny details, but for teachers and schools the minutiae of assessment processes matter.

## A timeline of curriculum and assessment changes

**1988**  First national curriculum and assessment levels introduced

**1999**  Revised national curriculum

**2007**  Assessing Pupils' Progress materials produced

**2011**  Bew report on Key Stage 2 testing, assessment and accountability

**2014**  New national curriculum comes into force

**2014**  Attainment levels removed

**2014**   National Association of Headteachers produces its own assessment frameworks

**2015**   Commission on Assessment without Levels reports

**2016**   Interim teacher assessment frameworks introduced

**2017**   Assessment frameworks for writing revised

# Implications of changes in curriculum and assessment

Recent changes in the curriculum and assessment have had an impact on the teaching of writing. The 1999 National Curriculum programme of study for writing (DfEE, 1999) balanced composition, process and transcriptional elements, and made explicit reference to breadth of study – children writing for a range of purposes, audiences and forms. Assessment was based on a set of levels, with children expected to reach level 1 by the end of year 1, level 2 by the end of year 2, level 3 by the end of year 4, and level 4 by the end of year 6. There were level descriptions and judgements were made using a 'best fit' approach. This approach led to difficulties in showing progress, particularly at Key Stage 2, and so the level descriptions were often modified by being broken down into sub-levels. These were then used to facilitate tracking of progress (although this too was not without its problems, giving an illusion of accuracy in assessment which might at times have been misleading). There were also concerns about the labelling of children as, for example, a 'level one writer' and the levelling of individual pieces of writing.

The assessment focuses of the Assessing Pupils' Progress materials (QCDA and National Strategies, 2007) were originally intended to move away from these practices. As with the programme of study, they were broad in scope and covered the main aspects of writing effectively. They were designed to sit between the programme of study and the level descriptions. Guidance on their use pointed out clearly that the different aspects were interdependent and each needed to be considered in relation to the whole text. There was also a strong statement that the focuses were assessment tools and not learning objectives. This distinction is a very important one; there is always a danger of assessment criteria becoming the focus of teaching, rather than being used as intended. The intention was to steer schools away from over-frequent levelling of all pupils, with the guidance that only a sample of children in each class needed to be assessed, and that the assessment should be periodic in order that there was a realistic chance of there being good evidence of progress. Practice, however, was often different, with all children being assessed using the APP grids on a very regular basis, and therefore the danger once again that there was insufficiently sound evidence of the progress that teachers were being pressed to demonstrate.

Although the APP materials have been replaced, they are worth examining because they present such a different picture of writing from that of the current assessment frameworks.

# APP Writing Assessment Focus

| AF1 | Write imaginative, interesting and thoughtful texts |
|-----|---------------------------------------------------|
| AF2 | Produce texts which are appropriate to task, reader and purpose |
| AF3 | Organise and present whole texts effectively, sequencing and structuring information, ideas and events |
| AF4 | Construct paragraphs and use cohesion within and between paragraphs |
| AF5 | Vary sentences for clarity, purpose and effect |
| AF6 | Write with technical accuracy of syntax and punctuation in phrases, clauses and sentences |
| AF7 | Select appropriate and effective vocabulary |
| AF8 | Use correct spelling |

In 2011, Lord Bew's review of Key Stage 2 assessment proposed a change to the statutory assessment of writing. The review suggested that as writing could not be tested as mathematics and reading were because of its creative element, it should be summatively assessed by teachers, rather than by external markers marking set writing tasks. The review also suggested a test of spelling, punctuation and grammar. These changes took effect in 2013.

The 2014 national curriculum made radical changes to the programme of study. The emphasis is very much on grammar, spelling and handwriting, where there is a significant amount of detail, while compositional aspects of writing and range are given a much lighter touch. For example, in year 1 children are expected to be able to *sequence sentences to form short narratives* (DfE, 2013, p. 24), but there is no suggestion that they might write in any other form. Poetry writing receives only one mention in the whole programme of study, in year 2. Changes to assessment were no less significant.

The removal of assessment levels in 2014 left teachers without an assessment system they were familiar with. The Commission on Assessment without Levels (DfE, 2015) stated in its report that levels were not being used in the way intended, and that using them to track progress, or to assess individual pieces of work, or to label children, was not helpful or appropriate, and had a negative impact on teaching and learning. There was a particular concern that such an approach had led teachers to 'teach to the test', with an undue focus on what children needed to do to reach a particular level. Indeed, 'uplevelling' was widely used to describe the process of focusing on or adding features to writing that would allow children to reach the next level, and classroom displays often explicitly promoted this. Nick Gibb, the schools minister, referred to this in a speech in 2015 in which he described seeing on a classroom wall a list of 16 words which were labelled as 'level 5 words'.

The disappearance of levels, however, left schools in a vacuum. No guidance was immediately forthcoming from central government, and although the final report of the commission eventually encouraged schools to develop their own approaches to assessment and indicated that the desire was to see a wide range of practice, there was understandable nervousness about developing forms of assessment and tracking that would be acceptable, particularly to Ofsted. The National Association of Headteachers (2014) therefore filled the gap by developing its own assessment framework, with its Key Performance Indicators and Performance Standards for each year group. These were based closely on the National Curriculum programme of study, and therefore were very heavily balanced in favour of transcriptional aspects of writing. In year 1, for example, two key performance indicators related to spelling, one to punctuation and one to handwriting, with only a statement about sequencing sentences to form a short narrative to represent compositional aspects of writing.

When the Standards and Testing Agency (2016) produced its own interim end of key stage assessment frameworks they too were weighted in favour of transcriptional aspects. Indeed, it is not beyond the bounds of possibility that a piece of writing could score well on all the indicators and yet be a poor piece of writing that does not engage the reader, or includes irrelevant information, or is badly organised – and equally possible that a piece of writing which is original or engaging or informative or funny, and which meets the primary purpose of writing, effective communication, does not meet the expected standard because of its punctuation and handwriting. This weighting has another significant danger – that teachers not only assess what they are asked to assess, but then prioritise these aspects in their teaching, meaning that content and style carry relatively little weight.

The recent tentative move back towards a 'best fit' model rather than the 'secure fit' approach was welcomed by the House of Commons Education Select Committee (2017). The exemplification materials (Standards and Testing Agency, 2017a, p. 4) contain the following significant statement:

> *Teachers can use their discretion to ensure that a particular weakness does not prevent an accurate judgement being made of the pupil's overall attainment in English writing. A teacher should still assess a pupil against all of the 'pupil can' statements within the standard at which they are judged, and a pupil's writing should meet all of the statements, as these represent the key elements of the national curriculum. However, a teacher's professional judgement takes precedence and this will vary according to each pupil.*

However, concerns over the emphasis on grammatical techniques remained, and a key concern of the Commission on Assessment without Levels (2015) remains: that an overall judgement does not represent performance in a meaningful way since it adds together a range of different aspects. Teachers make a judgement that children are working at the expected standard, working towards the expected standard or working at greater depth within the expected standard. There was also an issue with assessment based on 'can do' statements, since they may give the appearance of precision rather than actually offering it, and the Department for Education's teacher assessment frameworks use these. The concern about teaching to the test is, if anything, more acute than in the days of levels. The Commission's report also pointed out that self-assessment, increasingly seen as an important factor in children's progress, is dependent on a level of competence in what is being assessed. Year 4 children who are not altogether sure what a fronted adverbial is will not be able to make the judgement on whether their writing includes them, and may, for example, find it even harder to judge a more qualitative issue such as whether their use of pronouns aids cohesion while avoiding repetition.

# Moderation

Moderation is a process of ensuring that assessors make the same judgements of children's work. It is important that there is no variation between teachers in a school, or between different schools, or between local authorities who carry out the moderation of statutory assessment. Schools carry out regular moderation exercises, where pieces of work are considered by staff, and statutory assessment is moderated by the local authority, with 25 per cent of all schools being moderated each year (or more often if there are concerns). Moderators are trained and briefed, and carry out moderation exercises as part of their training to ensure that their judgements are secure; in this way, consistency is provided across the country.

To support teachers in making judgements, the Standards and Testing Agency (2017b) provides exemplification materials. These are collections of authentic writing samples from children who are working towards the expected standard, working at the expected standard, or working at greater depth. Each collection includes between six and eight samples, from a range of text types including both fiction and non-fiction. Contextual information is provided. Recognising that within the expected standard there will be a range of attainment, examples of children at the lower and higher ends of the range are included. In order to avoid unconscious bias, the pseudonyms used for the children are not recognisably girls' or boys' names. The samples are available both in the original handwritten version, without comments, and in typed format with annotations that analyse evidence for the judgements. These are categorised as C (composition), GP (grammar and punctuation) and T (transcription). There is also a summary statement explaining the overall judgement, and a table where each sample is matched to the 'pupil can' statements. For pupils working at the expected standard, the statements for greater depth are also considered, while for pupils working towards the expected standard, both the 'working towards' and 'working at' statements are considered.

The accompanying guidance (Standards and Testing Agency, 2017c and 2017d) gives good support for the process of making judgements – for example, teachers need to be aware that they should not be asking pupils to produce work specifically for external moderation, and that judgements should be based on 'day-to-day evidence' as well as the samples of work they gather – in other words, their knowledge of the child's writing more generally. The guidance also states that writing produced in subject areas other than English should be used for assessment purposes. There is also an explanation of what is meant by independent work – often a moot point – and the crucial note, discussed earlier, that 'a particular weakness' should not affect the overall judgement.

Teachers do not, of course, rely simply on external moderation to quality assure their judgements. Every time two teachers look at a piece of writing together and discuss it, moderation is occurring. These informal conversations complement the formal moderation meetings schools hold. It is important that we do ask constantly whether we are noticing the same things, interpreting them in the same way, and agreeing about ways forward. The more we can do this with as wide a range of professionals as possible, rather than one or two whom we regularly work with, the more confident we can be that our judgements are secure. However, there will always be an element of subjectivity, as suggested in the introduction, because in the end writing is judged in part according to the response of the reader, and our responses are based on our individual tastes and views.

# Conclusion

It is difficult to find an approach to summative assessment that meets all the requirements placed on it, while not having any negative side-effects, as was discovered in the nineteenth century when the 'payment by results' approach was introduced for elementary schools. This is not to say that there should be no attempt to track pupils' progress, but it is important, as has been suggested in previous chapters, to balance summative assessment with purposeful diagnostic assessment, in order to support that progress effectively. The concluding chapter will consider broader issues in the assessment of writing and possible ways forward.

# References

Bew, P (2011) *Independent Review of Key Stage 2 Testing, Assessment and Accountability: Final Report.* London: House of Commons.

Department for Education and Employment/Qualifications and Curriculum Authority (1999) *The National Curriculum Handbook for Primary Teachers in England.* London: DfEE/QCA.

Department for Education (2013) *The 2014 Primary National Curriculum in England.* Eastleigh: Shurville Publishing.

Department for Education (DfE) (2015) *Final Report of the Commission on Assessment without Levels.* London: Department for Education.

Gibb, N and the Department for Education (2015) *Assessment after Levels.* Available at: www.gov.uk/government/speeches/assessment-after-levels (accessed 28 June 2018).

House of Commons Education Select Committee (2017) *Primary Assessment Report.* London: House of Commons.

National Association of Head Teachers (2014) *Assessment Frameworks.* Available at: www.naht.org.uk/advice-and-support/curriculum-and-assessment/ (accessed 12 November 2017).

Qualifications and Curriculum Development Authority with National Strategies (QCDA) (2007) *Assessing Pupils' Progress.* London: DCSF.

Sellgren, K (2017) Teachers raise concerns over Sats marking. BBC, 11 July. Available at: www.bbc.co.uk/news/education-40567217 (accessed 18 June 2018).

Standards and Testing Agency (2016) *Interim Teacher Assessment Frameworks at the End of Key Stage 1 and Key Stage 2.* London: Department for Education.

Standards and Testing Agency (2017a) *2018 Teacher Assessment Exemplification: English Writing.* London: Department for Education.

Standards and Testing Agency (2017b) *Teacher Assessment Frameworks at the End of Key Stage 1 and Key Stage 2 for 2018/19 Onwards.* London: Department for Education.

Standards and Testing Agency (2017c) *2018 Key Stage 1 Teacher Assessment Guidance for Schools and Local Authorities.* London: Department for Education.

Standards and Testing Agency (2017d) *2018 Key Stage 2 Teacher Assessment Guidance for Schools and Local Authorities.* London: Department for Education.

# 13

# CONCLUSION: WHERE NEXT WITH THE ASSESSMENT OF WRITING?

## Feedback

Assessment, particularly of writing, has become a significant burden for many primary teachers. The detail and specificity of written feedback, which in some schools may be given for every piece of writing from every child, and the requirement in many schools to produce frequent summative judgements to evidence progress, have huge implications for workload. Atherton (2018) suggests that effective feedback promotes thinking, providing an indication of how the pupil is doing in relation to the goal, where to go next and how to get there. Doing this in a meaningful way is onerous and unlikely to be helpful if it is done on an almost daily basis, and where schools have decided to mix such intensive feedback with lighter touch marking, the task becomes much more manageable. Atherton (2018, p. 28) also points out that *well-designed group feedback* can be effective, stating that *feedback doesn't have to be perfect to have a positive impact*. Indeed, there is a growing interest in whole-class feedback as an alternative to individualised marking feedback; in this approach, the teacher reads a set of pieces of writing, noting strengths worth sharing with the whole class, common difficulties and so on, and the children then need to relate that feedback to their own work. Where the feedback indicates it is useful, follow-up activities can address aspects of the writing that many children needed to improve.

Conferencing is an approach in which teacher and pupil together review samples of the child's writing, evaluating it and discussing next steps. It has long been advocated as an approach to feedback that allows for considered discussion rather than written feedback which may not be understood, acted on or even read by the pupil. Finnis (2018) reports a school which gave up marking children's writing entirely, replacing written feedback with regular one-to-one conferences and brief written notes home to parents.

The introduction to this book raised the issue of formative as opposed to summative assessment, and suggested that too frequent summative assessment in order to attempt to demonstrate that children are making progress in writing from term to term, or even half-term to half-term, is problematic. Indeed, the changes in assessment practice that accompanied the curriculum change of 2014 were intended to move away from the approach of regular 'levelling' and to focus more on assessing whether children had mastered what had been taught in a unit of work. In terms of writing, for example, this might suggest assessing at the end of a unit of work on persuasive writing whether children were independently able to produce effective pieces of persuasive writing, which incorporated typical features of such writing and used them successfully. This would not be the same as simply assessing against generic criteria for writing. Progress would be harder to evidence, since the criteria would vary from one unit to another, but it would make the assessment much more relevant to the specific writing task. This seems more useful and more meaningful for children than constantly assessing against criteria that could apply to any piece of writing.

# Tracking progress

The approach of assessing attainment at the end of each unit of work does leave two questions to be answered. First, how can we demonstrate that children have made progress? Second, how can we know that teachers' judgements are in line with each other, both within schools and from school to school or area to area? The answer to the first could lie simply with a portfolio of the child's writing during the primary years. A sample from each term, including brief contextual notes, ought to show clear progress over time. The portfolio could perhaps feature one form, such as a story or a recount, repeated each year and the other two for each year demonstrating writing in a range of forms. Bearne and Reedy (2018) suggest that children might choose some of their own examples, and that the portfolio should be reviewed by pupil and teacher periodically. One would hope that without knowing in which year each had been produced, it would be possible to order them from the earliest to the latest. Where a form of writing such as instructions occurs in two or three different years, it should be obvious how the child's knowledge and skills have improved. Of course, the samples could be annotated, and marking grids devised, but this is not essential, and could in any case be added later or altered if needed, since the original piece would always be there to refer to. This is probably as meaningful as any complicated system of scoring and levelling, if not more so. A further advantage is that when children move on to secondary school, the writing record book can be sent home for families to enjoy and treasure. For young writers, even struggling writers in Key Stage 2, looking back at their first wobbly letters in the reception class gives them a real sense of how far they have come. Secondary schools are often quite open about the limited use they make of assessment evidence passed on from primary schools, and their preference for making their own baseline assessments, and they have the data from statutory end of key stage assessment.

Such an approach is attractively simple, avoiding the need for a number of judgements to be made, each of them often problematic in terms of the final decision as to whether the pupil 'can' or cannot do something. It also avoids the need then to put together all the judgements covering a number of very different aspects of writing to arrive at a final judgement, and doing all of this very regularly. It is in the spirit of the Commission on Assessment without Levels (DfE, 2015), which advocated a more radical approach to assessment than had developed under the old system of levels. It would free up time for more diagnostic assessment, which is more useful for planning and teaching, and is therefore more likely to lead to progress.

If this approach seems too minimalistic and does not offer the opportunity to generate data on progress, then tools such as the Writing Scale from the Centre for Literacy in Primary Education (2016) could be considered. The scale consists of six stages in writing development, from Early Writer, Developing Writer, Moderately Fluent Writer to Fluent Writer, Experienced Writer and finally Independent Writer. Along with the description of each stage, there is guidance on next steps and how to support children's development. The scale is intended to help teachers recognise and support progression, and not for summative assessment or as targets to move children on to the next stage. Bearne and Reedy (2018) have also developed a scale for tracking children's progress, the Scale of Progression in Writing/Composition, which outlines five stages in writing development, from inexperienced writer to *assured, experienced and independent writer*. The advice is that the scale should be used as a focus for discussion among teachers, and can be adapted to reflect the individual school's character and needs. Bearne and Reedy also provide a Scale of Progression in Multimodal Text Composition, which reflects the particular demands and opportunities of producing multimodal texts.

The comparative judgement approach (Pollitt, 2012) is attracting increasing interest in schools, and centrally, because it reduces the assessment workload, while being fast and reliable, and because it does not distort the curriculum. It relies on teachers' holistic professional judgements, since it is based on making a series of comparisons of pairs of pieces of writing, deciding simply which is the better, without reference to any pre-set criteria or marking scheme. With numbers of teachers making these judgements, rankings and measurement scales can be produced, and these can ultimately be used to measure progress.

# Self-assessment

The introduction raised the question of self-assessment and how well equipped pupils are to make judgements against the criteria they are often given, which necessitate a considerable level of subject knowledge. 'Real' writers do not evaluate their own writing according to whether they have used similes or fronted adverbials. They are often, however, realistic, if not harsh, in terms of whether their writing has achieved its purpose, whether they have said what they wanted to say, whether it reads well. There needs to be a careful balance between asking children to consider such broad questions and giving them a more specific focus for their reflections. Prompts for self-evaluation should move children towards being able to take control of this aspect of the writing process. Examples of such prompts might be as follows.

- What are we looking for in this type of writing?

- What do you think has worked particularly well in this piece of writing?

- If you were to make any changes now, what would they be?

- What were the hardest bits to get right?

- What did you want your reader to think/feel when they read this writing?

Bearne and Reedy (2018) suggest that children need to be taught to self-assess effectively and to practise the skill, and also to be involved in developing their own criteria.

Assessment of writing should also value pupil voice, as was argued in Chapter 1, and returned to in Chapter 11 in the context of children's writing at home. We often do not know enough about how pupils see the activity of writing in school, the place of writing in adult life and themselves as writers. What they say might not always be comfortable for us to hear, but it will inform our teaching, and allow us to find out how to make writing a more positive experience for pupils. And when children are confident and competent writers, writing itself gives them a voice. Writing provides an opportunity for children to express their feelings, views and ideas, and to display their knowledge, and this is empowering. Writing provides them with a permanent record of what they want to communicate, a way of making their mark on the world and to a wider audience. And it is precisely because writing is so challenging in terms of the range and sophistication of the skills involved that mastering it can give children so much satisfaction and pride.

# The purpose of assessment

Assessment is sometimes seen as the final stage of the planning and teaching cycle, rather than as what it is – the starting point as well as the end point, and also a continuous part of teaching. Effective planning depends on knowing what children need to learn next. During lessons, skilled teaching responds to what is happening – what children are finding difficult, what misconceptions are being revealed, what opportunities to develop learning present themselves. Assessment is not bolted on to teaching, it is integral to it. Drummond (1993) describes assessment as looking at learning and understanding what we see. It is hoped that this book has helped readers to understand better what they see when they read children's writing.

# References

Atherton, C (2018) *Assessment: Evidence-based Teaching for Enquiring Teachers*. St Albans: Critical Publishing.

Bearne, E and Reedy, D (2018) *Teaching Primary English: Subject Knowledge and Classroom Practice*. Abingdon: Routledge.

Centre for Literacy in Primary Education (2016) Reading and Writing Scales. Available at: https://clpe.org.uk/library-and-resources/reading-and-writing-scales (accessed 3 July 2018).

Department for Education (DfE) (2015) *Final Report of the Commission on Assessment without Levels*. London: Department for Education.

Drummond, MJ (1993) *Assessing Children's Learning*. London: David Fulton.

Finnis, A (2018) This Primary School has Abolished Marking in Favour of One-to-one Sessions with Teachers. *i News*, 18 July 2018. Available at: https://inews.co.uk/news/education/primary-school-abolishes-marking/ (accessed 29 July 2018).

Pollitt, A (2012) The Methods of Adaptive Comparative Judgement. *Assessment in Education: Principles, Policy and Practice*, 19(3): 281–300.

# INDEX

effective 158
importance of accurate ix
on poetry 68
on story writing 43
feelings, expression of 2, 161
fiction
adult judgement of 4–5
*see also* historical fiction; story writing
film reviews 46
fine motor skills 26, 29, 131
Finnis, A. 158
first person narration 32, 60, 87
first-hand experience(s) 41, 57, 61, 69
flashback structure 39
flow 83, 87
flowcharts 56, 58
formative assessment xi
framework for analysing early writing 20–1
free school meals, bias against children on xi
friendly tone, in persuasive writing 58
'frogs legs' pencil grip 129
fronted adverbials xi, 75, 83, 89, 90, 108

generic assessment tools x
generic writing skills 45
genres
reading different 41
vocabulary choice 93
working/experimenting with different 42–3
Gentry, J.R. 23, 113
girls, fashions in handwriting 134–5
glossaries 98
good writing 5, 9, 10
Grainger, T. 151
grammar xi, 90–1, 103, 154, 155
graphemes 23, 24, 25, 112, 115
gross motor skills 131
group feedback 158
guided writing 36, 68

Hall, N. 100, 101, 110
handwriting xii, 127–38, 154
assessment
checklist 137–8
early mark-making 21
letter formation 130–5
pencil grip and posture 128–30
statutory guidance 127
automaticity 128, 135, 138
consistency 127
difficulties 135–7
expectations of 127
fluency 128
importance of monitoring 128
importance in school 138

inconsistency in 135
individual styles 134–5
interventions 130, 131, 138
legibility 127, 137
poor 127–8
practising 137
quality of 127
speed of 127, 129, 135
highlighter pens 11
highly creative writers 5
historical fiction 4, 32
holistic judgements 160
home writing xii, 140–51
assessment 151
children's preference for 140
children's views on 151
choice in 143, 151
compared to school 143–4
encouraging 151
fragmentary nature of 142
homework 150
influence of school on 146
influences of reading 140–1, 142
production of a range of text types 144–7
homophones 112
hooks 32, 39, 56, 57
horizontal lines, in early mark-making 17
horror story writing 41
House of Commons Select Committee report
(2017) x, 155
*How the Elephant Got His Trunk* 42
humour 58
Huot, B. ix
hyphens 107

illustrations 50
imagery 70
imagination 43
'imitate, innovate, invent' 31
impact of writing, reflection on 68
imperative verbs 50, 51, 52, 60
independent writing 151, 156
individual handwriting styles 134–5
informal tone 60
information
additional, non-fiction writing 55, 59
gathering/selecting 49, 50, 54, 58, 98
information writing 46, 53–5, 65, 93
initial teacher training x
innovation, in story writing 31
instructions 50–3
intensifiers 3
introductions 49, 50, 53, 55, 57, 60
invented words 63
invention, in story writing 31, 35